Michael is an experienced company director and author for over 30 years. He has written several books and thousands of articles on gold, diamonds, bitcoin and blockchain, stem cell therapy and a plethora of other subjects.

Michael is the managing director of Technical Author Services Pvt Ltd.

Michael Moore

# A HANDBOOK FOR NEW COMPANY DIRECTORS

AUSTIN MACAULEY PUBLISHERS™
LONDON · CAMBRIDGE · NEW YORK · SHARJAH

Copyright © Michael Moore (2020)

The right of Michael Moore to be identified as author of this work has been asserted by him in accordance with section 77 and 78 of the Copyright, Designs and Patents Act 1988.

All rights reserved. No part of this publication may be reproduced, stored in a retrieval system, or transmitted in any form or by any means, electronic, mechanical, photocopying, recording, or otherwise, without the prior permission of the publishers.

Any person who commits any unauthorised act in relation to this publication may be liable to criminal prosecution and civil claims for damages.

Austin Macauley is committed to publishing works of quality and integrity. In that spirit, we are proud to offer this book to our readers; however, the story, the experiences, and the words are the author's alone.

A CIP catalogue record for this title is available from the British Library.

ISBN 9781528992909 (Paperback)
ISBN 9781528992916 (ePub e-book)

www.austinmacauley.com

First Published (2020)
Austin Macauley Publishers Ltd
25 Canada Square
Canary Wharf
London
E14 5LQ

# Table of Content

| | |
|---|---|
| **Introduction** | 7 |
| **Intro to Corporate Governance** | 8 |
| **A New Director** | 9 |
| **Functions of the Board** | 14 |
| **Cultural Lag of Boards** | 17 |
| **Unity in Diversity in the Boardroom** | 20 |
| **Risk Management** | 24 |
| **Time—A Weapon of Mass Construction** | 27 |
| **Discipline—the Secret to Success** | 32 |
| **Discipline is Basically** | 33 |
| **The Pareto Principle** | 37 |
| **Technology for Directors** | 41 |
| **What is Professionalism?** | 43 |
| **Reputation** | 45 |
| **Legal Issues for Directors** | 47 |
| **Corporate Responsibility** | 70 |
| **The Board's Code of Conduct** | 72 |
| **Corporate Governance** | 75 |
| **Basics of Business Networking** | 90 |
| **Customer Service** | 112 |
| **Reading Financial Statements for Directors** | 117 |
| **References** | 130 |

# Introduction

This booklet is designed for the new director. It gives a basic outline of the duties and responsibilities of a board director and includes some extra information to help the new director to find their way in a board and settle in it comfortably.

The board of director's function is primarily that of corporate governance. Corporate Governance is the method by which a corporation or organisation is governed or controlled. How it is run and administered and what policies and guidelines it operates from.

The type of governance a corporation has will depend on a number of factors. Size is one, both of the board and of the company. Ownership structure, even the power structure; who controls what. Also, the type of industry and community framework will have a bearing on the corporate structure and governance used by a company.

It is recommended that you study this book thoroughly and make it absolutely certain that you never go past a word, which you do not fully understand. The only reason a person gives up a study or becomes confused or is unable to learn is because he or she has gone past a word or phrase that was not understood. An attempt to read past a misunderstood word results in mental 'fogginess' and difficulty in comprehending the passages, which follows. If you find yourself experiencing this, return to the last portion you understood easily, locate the misunderstood word and get it defined correctly and then continue with the rest.

# Intro to Corporate Governance

Corporate governance has been defined by the ASX Corporate Governance council as:

"The framework of rules, relationships, systems and processes within and by which authority is exercised and controlled in corporations."

It also includes those methods by which companies and those directing and controlling the company, are held responsible for the company and can be therefore held accountable.

Companies come in all shapes, sizes and structures. The governance that applies will vary according to the type of company it is. A small two-director company with less than 10 employees and under one million dollars turn over will operate very differently to that of a large corporation of thousands of employees, a full board of 7 or ten directors with various committees and subcommittee and a turnover of billions of dollars.

In addition, public companies, unlike private, needed to conform to the Listed Rules for the Exchange, for ASX listed companies.

But the basics of corporate governance remain regardless of the size and type of company.

The directors must carry out, or ensure that the legal requirements of corporation are carried out and ensure that the corporation or company complies with statutory and common law, as applied to businesses.

# A New Director

A new director needs to become fully familiar with the fundamentals of the business and operations of the company. This includes making sure that one is fully informed about the company and its business. This can be done by making initial enquiries and doing some due diligence and research to ensure that this is a company which one wishes to participate in.

Becoming familiar with the financial operation and status of the company; including having the ability to read and understand financial statements and have a basic knowledge of accounting practice and material accounting standards, so that one has a thorough understanding of the company's financial capacity and solvency.

It means being able to understand financial reports and glean from them the existing and future condition of the company. It also means being responsible to ensure that accurate reports are presented under the Corporations Act, to satisfy legislative requirements and to query any inconsistencies or potential issues.

All directors are expected to attend board meetings, unless, exceptional circumstances such as illness prevents their attendance. Further, a director must be alert and pay attention to the matters being discussed at board meetings and should be aware that they cannot be excused from liability on the basis that he or she did not pay attention to the proceedings.

It is possible for a director to delegate responsibilities usually performed by the director. However, the director is still responsible for the supervision of the delegate and their activities whilst performing such duties and responsibilities.

These do not include signing off the final approval of accounts which must be done by the directors themselves.

The Corporations Act requires a director to act in good faith and in the best interests of the company and for a proper purpose. The interests of the company, in this wise, take precedence over individual interests. Duty is owned to the company, not to any particular individual. This includes encompassing the interests of the shareholders, to which the director has a responsibility, as it is their money the director is being responsible for.

In situations where there is one shareholder, which is the parent company, the director should keep in mind the interest of that parent company. The Corporations Act shows that a director is taken to act in good faith in the best interests of a wholly owned subsidiary if the subsidiary's constitution authorises the director to act in the best interests of the holding company, the director does so in good faith and the subsidiary is not insolvent.

The interests of creditors should also be taken into account, particularly if the company is insolvent or approaching insolvency.

A 'proper purpose' is where the purpose is to the benefit of the company. An example of an improper purpose is where the purpose would be to the benefit of the director or someone else, such as using knowledge of a company's new direction which, when publicly exposed, would affect the share price, for one's own benefit. In another example, directors issuing new shares for a collateral purpose, such as delivering control of the company to a particular person, ensuring that the directors remain on the board or obtaining some financial benefit for a director.

The Corporations Act also requires that a director cannot improperly use their position or information obtained because they are, or have been a director, to gain an advantage for them or others or cause detriment to the company. This includes not applying the company's property either for their personal benefit or for the benefit of another without the company's authority (usually requiring shareholder approval or constitutional authorisation) and not making an unauthorised use of confidential information belonging to the company.

A director needs to take care that he or she does not incur a conflict of interest, where they may discover profitable business opportunities as a result of their position within the company. Aside from the potential legal complications of such activities, there are also the moral issues as well as potential debarment for crossing the legal barrier.

It is far safer to regard all corporate property (including information) as company property and comply with the Corporations Act in this matter. In reality, only if a director can demonstrate that the property or information does not belong to the company or is otherwise public, will the director be free to make use of it.

The director is also obliged to prevent company insolvency as best he can. This can be done by being aware of the financial status of the organisation and bringing any issues to the attention of the board and requesting action to be taken to resolve such issues.

The Corporations Act also requires that directors do not participate in falsifying records and information and exposing such activity where discovered.

Indeed, there are specific provisions where the director may become personally liable to the company or a third party creditor for the amount of the debt and any loss or damage suffered by the creditor in relation to the debt because of the company's insolvency.

A director has certain defences. For example, he sincerely believes on reasonable grounds that the company was solvent or relied on information from a competent and reliable person whom the director believed, again on reasonable grounds, to be responsible for providing such information or did not participate on the management of the company due to illness and can show that he or she took all reasonable steps to prevent the company from incurring the debt.

In 2017, the Corporations Act was amended to provide directors with a defence to civil action for insolvent trading. "Directors will be afforded an exception from liability for insolvent trading, where the debt that the liquidator alleges had been incurred whilst the company was insolvent, was incurred in connection with a course of action that is reasonably likely to provide a better outcome for the company than the immediate liquidation or administration."

In addition, directors also have duties found in other legislation and which may impose significant personal liability on directors for a company's non-compliance. Such duties can be found in taxation laws, workplace health and safety laws, financial services legislation, environmental legislation and in trade practices regulations.

As has been demonstrated in the media under Australian Law, there are direct consequences for directors who breach their duties, including exposure to significant criminal and/or civil liabilities, or liability to pay compensation (damages) for a breach of their duties as a director.

Needless to say, the reputational damage to the director and even the company, as a result of such breaches, can be devastating.

A breach of duty or failure to meet any of their obligations may cause legal proceedings brought against them by any one of the companies itself, shareholders, regulators such as ASIC or the ACCC, third parties for misleading and deceptive conduct or anticompetitive behaviour, creditors and even insolvency administrators in the context of insolvent trading. If the breach is found to have been intentional, then the director is open to criminal liability as a result.

The Australian government recently increased the maximum penalties to 10 years' imprisonment and/or the larger of AUS $ 945,000 or three times the benefit obtained by the director, where an individual commits a serious criminal offence under the Corporations Act.

A directorship, as can be seen, is a big responsibility and is not to be taken lightly.

The following chapters are designed to assist the new director navigate this new territory and understand what he or she needs to know to become a qualified director whose contribution to the company is valued and appreciated.

# Functions of the Board

The board of directors of a company has very specific functions. The board of director's job is to manage or direct the management of the company, to steer and guide the company in achieving its objectives. This includes making sure the company adds value to itself. The company improves its performance by formulating the correct strategy and policies.

It also includes monitoring the performance of the company and ensuring that it is in the interests of the shareholders, so that it meets the goals and objectives of the company set, whilst complying with all the legal regulations and also managing risk effectively.

The board additionally has the duty of overseeing and monitoring the CEO and recruiting one where needed. They can also fire the CEO if they consider the CEO is detrimental to the company's interest.

In a very small company, the board might also be the management and take a 'hands on' approach. But by and large, the larger the company, the more the board will appoint management teams to apply the policies, strategies and objectives set by the board.

### The Board's Function is to:

- Appoint and monitor the performance of management to ensure that regulatory compliance is affected, to ensure that appropriate risk management is in place and above average performance is being achieved

- Ensure that the interests and value of the shareholders are correctly applied to improve the performance of the company
- Ensure that the relevant resources such as money, management, manpower and material are available
- Set a strategic direction that enhances and forwards the purpose, goals and targets of the company
- Monitor the performance of the organisation and the strategies that have been put in place. Set policies that enable management to apply and achieve the aims of the company
- Appoint a competent and effective CEO and having a succession plan

Most importantly, ensure that compliance with the various regulatory legal and accounting standards is in effect. This is where committees, for larger companies, can assist with monitoring and ensuring compliance with the various laws and guidelines imposed on companies and board members. The board has a duty to ensure the company is complying with the various regulations and there can be stiff penalties where a board would remiss in this activity. If a director cannot show they have done all they can to ensure legal compliance, then they can face fines or worse—imprisonment.

Setting the risk for the company is an important factor for the board to consider. Ensuring that the appropriate risk for each area is most important and a correct balance in managing risk between the board and the management team is vital. Some risks, say with mergers, large acquisitions etc., should probably be attended to by the board. However, lower level risks can be handled by the management team, although the board may and should want to be able to monitor risks, as it applies to the purposes and objectives of the company.

The board is accountable to the shareholders and should be reporting progress and matters of interest to the shareholders. These might include: the direction the board is taking with regard to the company, any change of direction, any acquisition or divestment of a significant asset and full disclosure of matters which the board consider, are significant to report to the shareholders. The board's functions could be boiled down to:

- Setting the culture for the company and ensuring it is in place and understood. Selecting an appropriate CEO and monitoring, evaluating and setting the remuneration and the removal, if found necessary, as well as setting and having a succession plan
- Ensuring communication facilities are in place with the various important stakeholders, such as shareholders, management, CEO, customers, clients, debtors and creditors of the company
- Having a network in place to effectively improve relations with other groups and individuals as they affect the company
- Putting into place, the appropriate risk management and monitoring it to ensure it is effective and there are no sudden surprises
- Making sure that appropriate governance process are in place and used by the board
- Making sure the company complies with the various regulatory bodies and the law
- Monitoring and controlling the company's performance
- Designing a big picture and having policy to forward it
- Having a 'crisis control policy' in place
- Formulating strategies and approvals

This is just an outline of some of the functions of a Board of Directors, most of which are gone into in some detail later. The main criteria, is that the board are conscious of their responsibilities as regards to the governance and duty of care, for the organisation they represent.

# Cultural Lag of Boards

There is such a thing as a cultural lag in the boardroom.

Company law requires boardroom decision making to be focused, but boardrooms tend to be pluralist by nature. Often the way business is done, business contexts and strategic decision making do change over time. Various factors bearing upon boardroom behaviour include inter alia preferences for the firm to act or to be seen to be acting in a socially and environmentally responsible manner: that is, to act ethically.

Conditions are more favourable for the emergence of a more widespread pursuit of social and responsible business within a safe and civil society.

Business Ethics: boardroom pressures in an age of moral relativism.

The slow take up of software, innovations, social networking, cloud computing challenges etc., long after they have been in use is a good illustration of cultural lag.

The term 'cultural lag' refers to the concept that there is a lag between the introduction of some innovation or new concept and the time it is taken on board. It does not necessarily apply only to technical innovation but can also apply to social changes as well as strategic and management changes. The term was first coined way back in 1922 by the noted sociologist William F. Ogburn in his work: *'Social change with respect to culture and original nature'*. His theory of cultural lag inferred that there is a period of maladjustment while the present culture is struggling to adapt to the new.

Usually one can see first, a resistance to the new culture. "We have always done things this way, no need to change" is often the catch cry. After a while, the resistance falls away, or perhaps in spite of the resistance or as a result of outside forces, the old culture eventually changes and 'catches up' with the new culture.

According to Ogburn, cultural lag is a common social phenomenon due to the tendency of material culture to evolve and change rapidly and voluminously while non-material culture tends to resist change and remain fixed for a far longer period of time. Due to the opposing nature of these two aspects of culture, adaptation of new technology becomes rather difficult. This distinction between material and non-material culture is also a contribution of Ogburn's work in 1922 on social change.

One example of cultural lag includes Dr Semmelweis's discovery of the cause and cure of childbed fever. For well over half a century after the discovery, women were still dying in agony after child-bearing. Eventually the culture caught up to it and an illness responsible for thousands of deaths was prevented. Dr Semmelweis's discovery was 'ahead of its time' and suffered a cultural lag. Other examples include motor cars, aeroplanes and many medical advances and not too long ago, stem cell research was widely resisted on moral and ethical grounds for many years, yet is now widely used.

So, cultural lag is not just a technological matter, it can relate to social and physiological and even psychological areas.

This can be quite apparent in the boardroom, as directors, who have been serving on a board for many years, struggle to adapt to new innovative ways of 'doing things'. How many boards are familiar with and can see the future potential of social networks for their company? A good example here is websites. The World Wide Web was initiated by Tim Berners-Lee in 1991 and from that point on, websites were able to be constructed and linked together. This opened the door to a presence on the internet. The first website was Info.cern.ch, (still going strong by the way) and others followed suit. But it was a long haul before many of the larger companies took up the option of a website. Even now, twenty years later, you can still find companies that have a cultural lag in this area and do not have a website.

Boards need to be very cognizant of the fact that there are new innovations and improvisations available on a regular basis and to look towards how these can be included in future planning. This particularly pertains to issues such as: green technology and the environment, the addition of women in the boardroom and health and safety issues, factors that have often been seen more as constraints, rather than ways to maximise shareholder value. This is a cultural lag, as eventually even these boards will be obliged to take up the slack here and incorporate such issues in their strategies.

Cultural lag is something that can be addressed. It does not have to be an emotive or socially resistive issue and, in many ways, reducing one's cultural lag, from a boardroom perspective, could place one in the forefront of competitors, which can only be beneficial for all stakeholders.

## Diversity in the Boardroom:

Unity in Diversity, Bhinneka Tunggal Ika[1], is the official national motto of Indonesia and it is a phrase that has been applied in many 'diverse' ways over many centuries and cultures. However, there is a particular importance to the phrase when it comes to the boardroom.

---

[1] Bhinneka Tunggal Ika is the official national motto of Indonesia. The phrase is Old Javanese translated as "Unity in Diversity," It is inscribed in the Indonesian national symbol, Garuda Pancasila (written on the scroll gripped by the Garuda's claws) and is mentioned specifically in article 36A of the Constitution of Indonesia.

# Unity in Diversity in the Boardroom

Many different skills and experiences are drawn upon in the boardroom in search of the exact strategy required to ensure a flourishing and prosperous company. As well as the obvious financial skills required, there are various other skills which a board might feel is needed to operate that particular board successfully.

Strategy is a key component of a board's activity, for example and how this is applied will depend on the type of company it is and a number of different skill sets, which it may need to be brought to bear on particular issues. A mining or exploration company, for example, would look for a different mix of skills than a financial-based or retail sector company. A larger board may need a larger, diverse set of skills to set the strategy for a national or international company. A small board may be more 'hands' and so require a different and possibly more closely aligned set of skills. A NFP (Not for profit) board, as suggested, requires quite a different set of skills. Fund raising, for example, is likely to be a prominent skill with a NFP organisation.

So there can be a very diverse set of skills, knowledge and experience required, depending on the type and size of company.

Some important questions arise here: just how diverse should the directors of a board be? How many members of a board constitute the optimum number for that board? When is there enough diversity? And could there be in fact, a case of too much diversity for a board?

## Diversity of skills VS number of board members:

The ages-old question arises here. How many directors does it take to change a light globe? Or in other words, how many directors does a board need to operate at optimum efficiency and ability?

An old, Thespian mentor, whom I once knew in the Theatre, once said to me: "The best committee is a committee of one." Of course, he meant that decisions can be made far easier and there is less likely to be procrastination with a smaller number of people in the decision-making process. The smaller the board, the easier it is to get issues and questions resolved and strategies planned. But strategies can fall short if there are insufficient skills and experiences at the board level. A board has to then strike a balance between the need for a diversity of skills and the number of directors on a board. Too few and the board suffers from a lack of skills, knowledge and experience (SKE). Too many and the board can become overweight and sluggish and the ability to develop optimum strategy and make timely decisions can suffer.

So what is the optimum number of board members? Outlining a clear definition may assist in determining the answer to that question.

## Definition of Optimum Directors for a Board:

The quantity of directors with the right diversity of skills, knowledge and experience necessary to provide fit and proper governance and in which the other board members can trust.

Which then brings us to an important issue of trust within the boardroom.

## Trust in other board members skills:

With a diversity of skills on a board, trust becomes paramount. If all the board members have the same skills, knowledge and experience (SKE) necessary to perform the board functions, only one board member would be required. It is because they do not, that a diversity of SKE is required. And the more diverse and the more board members there are, wider the level of trust will be needed.

Trust in other board members and their skills are vital. How do we know if we can trust them? How much do we trust them? Of course, much of this is established when a board member is taken on board, so to speak.

Interviews are done; the establishment of the skill, knowledge and experience the prospective board member can bring to the board. Will the director be a good 'fit' and can he or she integrate and work smoothly within the board and with the other board members? All these and many other questions determine if a prospective director will integrate with the rest of the board.

On one level, each member carries the same responsibility of every other member and the board as a whole.

On another level, no individual board member can be expected to have the same experience and skills of every other board member, so picking the right mix of diversity for a board is paramount in order to ensure that trust can be afforded by each board member, in the other board members.

In other words, the more a board fits together well, the more effective it will be. Developing bonds and collaborating together can make a tremendous difference to the board's effectiveness.

Would the proper fitting and effective diversity have saved Hardie (James Hardie Industries plc. is an industrial building materials company, headquartered in Ireland and listed on the Australian Securities Exchange which specialises in fibre-cement products. James Hardie manufactures and develops technologies, materials and processes for the production of building materials and has had a long term court issues with employees and their asbestos operation over many years). The fact that it was not 'saved', tends to suggest that the diversity of skills, knowledge and experience (not to mention the trust), between board members was not optimum.

With the regulations for board members becoming ever tighter and more restricting, boards will need to fine-tune the number and diversity of their board members to ensure they have a fit that is optimum for that board and in which trust can also fit safely within the board.

# Risk Management

What is Risk Management?

## A Good Definition of Risk is:

"The possibility of loss, injury, disadvantage or destruction."

Manage, according to the New World Dictionary, is defined as:
"V.t. to guide or handle with skill or authority; control; direct."

Management is a noun. So Risk Management could be defined as:
The practice with processes, procedures, methods and tools of handling, of controlling risks in a project or activity, function or business with a view to the reduction of those risks to an economically acceptable level Risk Management provides a disciplined environment for proactive decision making to:

- Assess continuously what could go wrong (risks),
- Determine which risks are important to deal with,
- Formulating strategies for reducing those risks,
- Implementing the strategies to deal with those risks,
- Recording and maintaining information for management analysis.

This includes identifying a concern that could translate into a potential risk. What activities could constitute a risk in your business? Could it be the fact that you accept credit cards online? Could it be the level of service you are offering your clients? Is there a potential problem with the products you are offering? What level of Quality Management do you employ? How responsible is your staffs in dealing with clients and/or products?

Risk Management – Determine which risks are important to deal with Identifying concerns are an important factor and precede identifying risks as to potential and consequences.

The options for assessing the risks need to be employed and priorities should be set. Some risks may be relatively low priority, such as the risk of a client complaining about waiting five minutes on the phone to speak to someone. But the risk of a fraudulent credit card being used to purchase a AUS $1000 item may be quite high. This is something to make a serious assessment on.

## Formulating Strategies for reducing those Risks:

From this, risk management plans and procedures may be developed and if needed, presented to senior management for authorisation. What policies and procedures do you need to put into place to reduce the risk of say…the AUS $500 credit card fraud?

Implementing the strategies to deal with those risks:
Having a process or procedure in place, which is followed by the company and its employees. This might be a verification process for credit cards, for example. Or it could be an investigative procedure for a complaint about the company products or service.

Recording and maintaining information for management analysis

A record of activities and results of the risk management undertaken for effective analysis, control and future accuracy of risk management is vitally important. Is there some policy you need to formulate as a result of a particular complaint or fraud, for example, that took place and which illustrates a deficiency in the quality of product or service or the security arrangements?

Risk Management, therefore, is the route by which you discipline yourself when it comes to dealing with various issues, such as complaints and fraudulent activity. The guidelines outlined here give you a framework you may use to formulate effective strategies to cover many potential issues that could impede your business progress and expansion.

Attention to risk management will depend largely on the size of the company. In a larger company, management may do risk assessment on some matters and the board would be more concerned with risk associated with major acquisitions and or divestments.

# Time—A Weapon of Mass Construction

"Time is nature's way of preventing everything happening all at once?"

– Anon

It has been said, that you are born with a lifetime ahead of you and when you die you have run out of time. In between, it is a battle to get everything you want done in time.

Advertisers scream, that by using their products, you can save time. Yet, there is no time bank in which to save it.

Did you see that car in the street speed by? Is that time? It left point A and then, after a time, it arrived at point B. Have you ever felt that you were watching time pass you by?

Did you ever have a short nap and it seemed like an eternity, while you were dreaming and when you woke, only two minutes had passed?

Have you noticed that time slows down in proportion to boredom and speeds up in proportion to enjoyment?

Is time really that flexible or does it just seem like it?

And if time is money, the unemployed should be wealthy, since they have so much of it and the very industrious should be poor, since they have so little of it. A fallacy, of course, since everyone from the most wealthy to the abject poor all have precisely the same amount of time in a day as anyone else.

Many moons ago, when I was a young man, I worked in a factory and observed 'Time & Motion' experts walk around the factory at periodic intervals. They would watch an assembly worker put a widget into a thingamajig. They would watch very carefully and noted how long it took for the worker to move his arm to pick up the widget and place it on top of the thingamajig and bang it in. Place the thingamajig to his left and then reach over to his right to pick up the next widget.

Click would go the stopwatch.

After a time out, would come an edict, that "placing widgets in thingamajigs will now only take 1.25 minutes."

This became so unpopular that after a couple of years they changed their name to 'Particle Flow Analysts'.

The stopwatch remained the same, however. This technique of saving time because 'time is money' failed, not only because of union protest or because the watcher was just, watching time, but because they were making the unwitting assumption that their workers were robots and could be made to work as such.

Time is certainly that elusive something, hard to get a grip on.

So how do you manage time?

Let's change our thinking. Let's think not in terms of wasting time, watching time or saving time.

Let's think instead, in terms of creating time.

How do you create time?

"I'm late…I'm late…for a very important date…," said the white rabbit in Lewis Carroll's 'Alice in Wonderland'.

Can you create time? Yes you can. You will be happy to know!

The way to create time is to take control of time. That is…YOU take control of time.

How do you do that!

The answer is PSAP

PRIORITIES
SCHEDULING
ACTION
PREDICTION

## Priorities:

The first step to using time, is to set priorities for the activities you have to do.

A young, aspiring violinist was having trouble reaching the level she desired. "I just don't have enough time to practice as much as I should. There are things to be done in the house: cleaning, laundry and I have to work," she complained.

Her teacher said, "Why don't you change your priorities?"

"How do you mean?" the young concert violinist asked.

"Why don't you practice daily first, then do your household chores. Which is more important to you?"

That young girl took her teacher's advice and went on to become a first violinist in an orchestra. She rearranged her priorities.

How could you rearrange your priorities? Are you doing unimportant things as a first priority and leaving the most important matters last?

## Scheduling:

The second step is scheduling. Not just ordinary scheduling, but creative scheduling. Now this is not like creative accounting. Creative scheduling could also be called cramming scheduling. The idea is to cram as much as you can, in a week, day, hour or minute, as possible.

When do you get the most done? When you're busy!

A lazy day: you have nothing to do. A good day to mow that lawn, perhaps, paint that fence, write up that report for old so and so.

But what do you do? Nothing!

A busy day: you have five appointments in the morning, a report to type up and two meetings to attend. How can you ever get it done?

But you do. You rush around, going from one meeting to another. Dash off that report, interview those five people and lo' and behold, it's lunchtime!

What is the difference? The difference is that you were busy. Years ago, I had a girlfriend who was one of the nicest ladies you could wish for. But she had no time. She would get up in the morning, and by the time lunchtime came around, she was still not ready to go out. Her kitchen was always full of unwashed dishes, clothes strewn around the apartment. Ask her to go out and she was 'too busy'.

"I don't have enough time," she would say. Yet she did nothing. She did not have to work. Yet, what did she DO all day, I never could figure out for a long time, until I realised that she had no schedule, did not complete anything she did. Oh she would start things okay, start this, and start that. But she never finished anything. There were more incomplete activities than you could throw a stick at. She had no schedule.

Fill up your appointment book. "Oh I am not a salesperson," you cry.

"Well you have appointments with yourself too. Do those exercises. Write that report. Eat that lunch on time. Do your study. Do this. Do that. List them all down."

"That's crazy. I cannot do all that in a day," you cry. Yes you can! If you want something done, give it to a busy man. Turn it around. If you want to do something…get busy!

## Action:

You knew it would come, didn't you?

Action. Apply your schedule. Stick to it. Adhere to it like glue. Become one with your schedule.

Under action, there is COMPLETE EVERYTHING YOU DO. Under no circumstances are you to leave something undone or incomplete or unfulfilled or half-done.

If an activity appears too big to be completed, break it up into smaller activities. How do you eat an elephant? One bite at a time!

There is power in this activity. It is easy to become distracted when you have a heap of things to complete and your attention is dispersed over all those incomplete activities you started but never got around to finishing.

Action is COMPLETING the actual activities on your schedule in the priority you have assigned to completion.

This is the nugget of PSAP.

YOU set the priority!

YOU work out the schedule!

YOU do the actions!

And YOU will have the prediction!

## Prediction:

The prediction is the result you desire and expect. It is the result of accumulation of your hard work and effort. It is the goal you fully know you will achieve, as a result of PSAP. It is what you know will occur, if you perform certain functions. It is not following the stars in the hope that things will work out. What if that star goes supernova?

No, it is YOUR effort and hard work pursuing your goal using Priorities, Scheduling, Action and Prediction to knowingly attain your goals with malice aforethought!

It is what you KNOW will happen, because you have followed the principles here and done the time and done the work.

It is your reward to wealth and happiness.

And it did not take that much time after all did it?

# Discipline—the Secret to Success

What is discipline and how can it be used as a tool? Discipline has quite rightly been called the application of responsibility to action in the direction of achievement. Sounds very scholarly, but it is also very true. There is a secret to discipline. It has the astounding ability to make one very successful in any endeavour of life.

### The Foundation of Success:

"Discipline is the foundation upon which all success is built. Lack of discipline inevitably leads to failure."

– James Rohn.

Discipline has often come to be regarded as a dirty word by some people. Perhaps the connotations of strict drill sergeants and school masters have coloured, what is perhaps the most useful and effective tool available to achieving what you want.

# Discipline is Basically

DO IT.

Whatever it is you want to do or want to achieve, or want to have in life.

DO IT.

Discipline is simply not stopping, but continuing.

When you are tired, or fed up, or hungry, or your feet hurt. Or you still hunger for that cigarette or drink. Or you feel lazy, want a holiday, just feel it's too much or just feel like a sickie[2] or want to spend that AUS $100 shopping instead of saving it, as you promised yourself, discipline is where:

YOU STILL DO WHAT YOU HAVE TO DO ANYWAY.

## Discipline Is Not Giving Up

Discipline is being responsible for doing something…anyway.

If you adopt the attitude that discipline is a tool and not a chore, you will discover how useful discipline can be.

Speak to any winner, any sports personality who has climbed the ladder and he or she will tell you that discipline is the bridge between his or her goal and the accomplishment of that goal.

The top golfers of the world like Jack Nicklaus, Greg Norman, Tiger Woods will hit upwards of 1000 golf balls a day, practicing, day in day out. Even if they do not feel like

---

[2] Australian slang for a sick day off work

it, or have an 'off' day. There they are hitting balls one after another. Rain or shine. Heat or hot, wet or dry. Discipline.

How many lengths of the pool do you think an Olympic Gold Medal winner like Michael Phelps swims each day, day in day out? How many slam dunks do you think Michael Jordan did each day in practice to maintain his peak performance? How many hits did Don Bradman take a swing at to become such a legend?

It is discipline and persistence, come what may, not luck or good fortune that makes the difference between a winner and a no winner.

Discipline can take you to success. Discipline could be called the application of determination to achieve a known goal, despite any and all personal obstacles.

If you are determined that you must put away AUS $100 per week, towards a property investment, for example, discipline is the tool to ensure that you do it and don't use the AUS $100 for a night out or to purchase that whoozit you have been aching to get.

If you don't put that AUS $100 away this week, that's AUS $100 you are delayed in reaching your goal. It is easy to say. "Oh that was just one day, I'll start again tomorrow."

The next week, there is another bill coming in, "I'll just pay that bill now. There is a sale on. One more week won't hurt. I'll start this program next week." It does hurt! You goal will recede further and further away into the distance, until it disappears. This is procrastination at its worse and procrastination is the covert enemy of discipline.

If you look around you, you will see that nature employs discipline. The tree strives and reaches higher and higher towards the sunlight despite the relentless pull of gravity. The tree does not have a sickie or a day off.

A Weed will push up through the concrete. The concrete is harder than the weed but the weed has something the concrete does not have: Determination without end. Insects, animals and fish, all strive better, despite the odds or opposition to achieve better survival for themselves and their offspring. Instinct you might say. Survival, perhaps? Well, whatever you want to call it, it is still a case of not giving up but persisting until the goal is reached.

It is all very nice practicing affirmations such as, "I will be wealthy." It has no value without the goal to aim for, the plan to show you the route, the action of travelling along that route and the discipline to get you there. Besides which, that is just another way of putting it in the future. Tomorrow never arrives as it is always today. It is what you do here and now, today, that decides your future, not what you intend to do tomorrow.

It takes more than just saying, "I'm gonna be rich." It takes applying oneself to a known plan of action in a known direction towards a specific goal with no deviation from the path. Discipline is bound up with responsibility and integrity, rather like a triangle. Taking responsibility for oneself is the application of discipline. Can you take responsibility for your chosen path even if the way becomes difficult?

Thomas Macaulay's definition of integrity was, "The measure of a man's real character is what he would do if he would never be found out." Worth thinking about. Can you apply discipline when there is no one around to check on you? That is a true measure of discipline.

Tom Hirshfield, the Physicist said, "If you hit the target every time, it is too near or too big." Discipline is not giving up but persisting anyway.

Any failure you experience along the way is simply part of the journey, not the end of the journey. All successes are built on failure. Failure might be the first step. Success is the last for those with the determination and discipline. Edison tried 1000 times, before he hit success with the incandescent bulb. Ray Bradbury submitted 1000 stories to publishers before he got one published. J. K Rowling was rejected by no less than 12 publishers before Bloomsbury Publishing took her on with the Harry Potter story, 'The Philosophers Stone'. Now she is a world-famous author and she and the publishers are worth millions. Philip Knight, CEO of NIKE once said, "The only time you have to succeed, is the last time you try." So do not expect to necessarily get it right the first time and don't consider yourself a failure when you don't. It can take practice and perseverance.

That is where the discipline comes in. Discipline can be made a habit.

There are many in the property field that have seen the results of applying discipline. Anthony Barakat, the Brisbane property investor, now worth an estimated 157 million dollars. Phillip Wolanski, in property, worth 160 million dollars. Ian McMullen and Family, also in property and worth a cool 211 million dollars. There are many more. All started out with next to nothing and all applied discipline as a tool to help them on their way.

So the results of applying discipline can be absolutely staggering. When you achieve your goal and have applied discipline along the way, come what may, imagine how strong and capable you will feel. There is enormous satisfaction to be gained by achieving one's goals through discipline properly applied.

Assuming responsibility for yourself by being persistence in reaching your goal, despite any obstacles that try to impede you. Maintaining your vision and looking at the goal and not the obstacle.

Keeping discipline by doing whatever has to be done even when you don't want to do it and being true to yourself are all part of a winner's attitude and a wealthy one too.

Practice using discipline. Treat it like a friend. Become excited about it! If you miss from time to time, okay, start again. Persist. You secretly know you can. Take a smaller step if a bigger one is too much. Take lots of small steps. Practice using discipline, it can make you a fortune!

There are ten little words that demonstrate what it comes down to:

If it is to be it is up to me.

Apply those ten little words and discipline and who knows where you can end up?

# The Pareto Principle

"Principle: You cannot overestimate the unimportance of practically everything."

– John C. Maxwell,
Developing the Leader within You.

Robert K McKain said, "The reason most major goals are not achieved is that we spend our time doing second things first."

When running a business, it is easy to become distracted by the mundane and petty things around us. It is all too easy for our attention to become trapped in something insignificant and let our focus gets pulled away from what is important. Setting priorities in our activities is one way by which we can ensure that we stay on track. Look at how your activities and actions assist or impede your progress towards expansion. Your time is valuable. Look at how much of it is spent working on achieving your goals and how much is not. On April $14^{th}$, 1912 a great ocean liner, The Titanic sank. One interesting story which emerged from that event concerns a woman getting into a lifeboat suddenly stopped and, turning around, rushed off, stepping over money and jewellery scattered on the decks. She reached her cabin and, ignoring her own jewellery grabbed some oranges, rushed back to the lifeboat and jumped in. A dramatic shift in priority when an emergency arrives.

Determining a priority will depend on what your goal is at a particular time. The goal of the woman on the Titanic was to survive the open sea. She adjusted her priorities to fit her goal.

## What Is The Pareto Principle?

The Pareto Principle is a method of isolating your time, money, activity or priorities in such a way that you are able to increase those things that will assist you in achieving your goals quicker while at the same time decreasing those things which would impede or stop your progress towards the accomplishment of your goals. It is also known as the 80/20 principle. It describes a ratio of one thing to another. Many sales people know it well and are taught it in the early stages of their sales training. Basically it demonstrates that 20% of your time, activity, money, etc. will produce 80% of your results.

Here are some examples:

20% of your work will produce 80% of your results

20% of your money will produce 80% of your profit

20% of a book will contain 80% of the content

20% of the people will eat 80% of the food

20% of the people will have 80% of the money

20% of the products will produce 80% of the profit

20% of your customers will be responsible for 80% of your profit

20% of your customers will produce 80% of your complaints

20% of your orders are more likely to be fraudulent orders

And the other way round.

80% of your work will produce 20% of your results

80 of your money will produce 20% of your profit

80% of a book will contain 20% of the content

80% of the people will eat 20% of the food

80% of the people will have 20% of the money

80% of the products will produce 20% of the profit

80% of your customer will be responsible for 20% of your profit

80% of your complaints will come from 20% of your customers

80% of your fraud problems will come from 20% of your orders Sales people know that 80% of their time is spent getting 20% of their sales and 20% of their prospects result in 80% of their commission. The exercise they are constantly engaged in is locating those 20% type of prospects to increase their commission.

A business understands that 80% of their profit comes from 20% of their customers. Their task is to either make the other 80% of their customers produce the same ratio of income as the 20% do, or to reduce the 80% that only produce the 20% profit or change them for the 20% type of customers that produces the 80% of their profits.

Imagine what would happen if 80% of the time, energy and money you spend on unproductive issues, reduced to 20%? What a difference that would make!

According to John C. Maxwell, in his book, *Developing the Leader within You*, 20% of your priorities will give you 80% of your production IF you spend most of your time, energy, money and personal attention on that 20%.

Use the Pareto Principle to isolate that 20% of your priorities will reduce your losses the most. This means putting into place policies, processes and procedures that will effectively reduce those handicaps to the irreducible minimum.

For example, categorizing complaints will help you to locate areas of your business which require the most attention. Perhaps 80% of your complaints come from long delays on the phone. Correcting this with a change of policy on how clients are handled by phone would result in an 80% drop in complaints in this example.

Isolating those successful actions which resulted in a sudden increase in business; perhaps a special discount offered or a particular phasing in your advertising, could result in an increased flow in business thereby.

Discovering that 80% of the communications in the company are a waste of time due to the same communications being bounced around with no result and putting in place processes to ensure this does not happen can reduce the amount of company time wasted. Even one's own inbox, incoming communications or documents, for example. Picking up a document or paper and actually handling it on the spot rather than putting it down again with the thought *'I will handle that later'*, will reduce wasted valuable time and energy, as the matter will not then require handling twice.

There are many examples of how the Pareto principle can be used, even for directors. If you are in a board meeting to resolve some issue, resolve the issue, do not put it off for a later meeting.

# Technology for Directors

I recently attended a business luncheon with a panel of experts on the subject of 'Technology for Directors' and discussed a broad range of issues relating to a director's and board's approach and strategy in the field of technology. Although the questions and discussion was informative and enlightening, I felt that, due to time constraints, there were some important issues not gone into depth. One if these were the fuzziness that surrounds the formulation of strategy and the decision making process with regard to technology and technological innovation and application. Many boards confuse strategy with the application of IT within their company almost to the point of a, "Well, you understand that sort of thing, you take care of it," approach.

Although the decision-making process, with regard to implementation, is correctly regarded as in the province of the CIO and IT executives, some boards relegate the strategy to the CIO and IT team also causing the control of the strategy to fall outside the boards control and resulting in errors and mistakes, sometimes of magnitude.

The difference between the strategy formulation and the implementation technology needs, for some boards, to be clearly delineated and boards have a responsibility to understand the technology that applies to their company in order to effectively formulate the strategy required to steer the technology, which is a tool after all, in a direction that enhances the company's purpose and goals.

Once the strategy is determined, then the executive decisions by the CIO and others that translate the strategy into the correct application can be effected.

Another issue, which the panel touched lightly on, is where a board or board members, are under time constraints and over committed tend to leave direction of IT matters to the CIO and the executives and have a tendency to rely on the IT personnel themselves to provide governance. While boards may traditionally seek external advice and consultation in legal, financial and HR matters. This rarely occurs with IT matters and in this can be a big error on the part of boards.

Important areas the director should be aware of where this applies include:

Security of information including the safeguarding of company assets and confidentiality,

Fraud prevention and being conscious of safeguards to prevent fraud and criminal activity,

Marketing through electronic means, such as social media and public media.

# What is Professionalism?

We all seem to know what professionalism is, but in the overabundance of enthusiasm in which we attack our areas of interest, the application of professionalism can get left by the way side from time to time.

## A Good Definition of Professionalism is:

Acting in a manner consistent with the expected codes of conduct, for the profession that one is representing.

If one were to act and to be perceived to act in a professional manner, one would firstly need to understand what is expected of him or her.

What follows is some criteria or guidelines for a professional code of conduct, not just to the general public, but also towards one's peers since that also reflects upon our character and our adherence to professional values.

Firstly, do not act in a manner that gives others the impression that you are an amateur. This means not just dabbling in the profession or activity you are engaged in. Find out all there is to know about the subject and study it until you know it cold. Adopt the frame of mind that everything you do you do as a professional.

This means in any situation you handle as a professional anything that arises. You adopt a professional viewpoint and act from that viewpoint.

Being professional includes understanding that one is not just the representative for the profession one is engaged in, but the ambassador of that profession also. Therefore one should understand what is expected of one, not just as a professional but also as an ambassador for one's profession.

Maintain a professional level of communication with the public and with one's peers in the profession. This would include respecting other members of the profession as professionals, regardless of any provocation or apparent excuse to the contrary, and demonstrating the ability of restraint when provoked into being unprofessional in one's response and attitude regardless of the source.

Maintaining a high ethical code of financial conduct that is reflected in one's records and demonstrates high level of honestly

Acting in a manner that does not include denigrating peers or the public, privately or publicly, but maintaining an exemplary standard of communication that demonstrates one's professionalism level Provide an exemplary level of service that never fails to impress in all aspects to one's clients, customers, peers and others so that the collective reputation of the profession for service is enhanced and it's future assured as a result.

Physically present oneself in the manner expected for the profession or business. This would include the appropriate dress code for the occasion.

What are the benefits of having and following a professional code of conduct?

# Reputation

Reputation is a perception. A good definition of reputation is the estimation in which one is held character in public opinion; the character attributed to a person, thing, or action; repute.

Are you well-thought of by your customers and your business associates? Is your reputation a valuable commodity or is it somewhat tarnished?

A business can rise and fall on its reputation. A whisper in the share market. False rumours spread around and other deliberate attempts to thwart a company's business with false public complaints can put any company in jeopardy. With the internet particularly and with the easy public broad issue of statements now available, a reputation can be tarnished and even destroyed almost overnight. Businessmen have even been known to take their lives when their reputation is impugned. How much value do you put on your reputation?

Your reputation is enhanced when you can follow the guidelines above.

As will be mentioned later, integrity forms a major part of professionalism. Thomas Macauley once said, "The measure of a man's real character is what he would do if he would never be found out."

Let's say you find a wallet stuffed full of dollar bills on a lonely road. The wallet has the name and address of the owner who could very well be a little old lady. You could keep the money and throw the wallet away. Who would know? Or, you could return the wallet with the funds intact.

Here are two levels of integrity. Which do you think would demonstrate your real character?

The answer will tell you what you consider your level of professionalism is. If you are known for your persistency in following a strict code of ethics in business, then your integrity will remain intact. This will enhance the trust others place in you immeasurably. Including the above guidelines in your professional conduct will demonstrate your level of integrity to observers.

### Trust:

Apart from the legal definitions of trust, the common meaning can be defined as: "the acceptance of a person or activity without any further verification."

The dictionary definition is: "to place confidence in, to rely on, to confide, or repose faith in."

It could be said then, that written contracts are those things that are there when trust is not. In the diamond industry transactions between dealers are on a "my word is bond" basis. A shake of the hand and the deal is done. Afterwards, the paperwork is completed but the deal is done on a trust basis in the first instance. The ideal of betraying that trust is unthinkable in that environment.

To earn or gain trust is to be predictable in one's integrity and to offer up to follow an agreed upon set of guidelines which are acceptable to the public and one's peers. Scrupulously following the above, therefore, is likely to raise one's professional status with the public and one's peers to astronomical heights with consequent improvement in one's reputation and ethical peace of mind!

# Legal Issues for Directors

According to the Australian Institute of Company Directors (AICD): "Directors must ensure legal risks are assessed and that a compliance program is developed and working," in order to ensure legal compliance is affected. Therefore, although a director is not expected to know all the laws pertaining to his company, at least an understanding of the legal environment in which a company operates is demanded.

If any legal issues arise that can impact on the company and, indeed the directors, then the court will take into account the compliance measures put into place, or not, by the directors. This means that an active culture of directors aware of the corporate responsibility their office holds to ensure legal compliance should be in place.

A passive, or non-acting, director will not be an excuse for any later found illegal activities or legal noncompliance as has been evidenced in recent times. Organisations such as Enron, among many others spring to mind.

### Example:

A company policy that simply says, 'our company will comply with the trade practices act', is insufficient and a compliance program of staff training, education on the relevant legal matters, implementation, monitoring and sanctions must be, not only in place, but seen to be in place. A culture of active compliance should be present and visible and the director(s) have a responsibility, in the words of Capt. Picard, to "make it so." Corporate culture is defined as: "That attitude, policy and rule, course of conduct or practice that exists within the body corporate generally or in the body corporate in which the relevant activities take place."

Directors should understand that although it is prudent to seek and acquire legal advice, such legal advice does not absolve the director of legal liability for the company which he, or she, represents. It merely shows that legal risk is acknowledged and does not demonstrate actual activity on the part of the director to ensure legal compliance. That would require a compliance conduct, as indicated before, to be in place. Any legal advice is obtained purely for the benefit of the company and would not take into account the benefit of a competitor, say, or even clients and creditors. So it does not absolve the director of any complacency in legal issues that relate to other parties where the other party is illegally disadvantaged.

Ultimately, it is the director that takes responsibility for the actions of the company in terms of legal risk assessment and the legal actions of the company.

The legal framework each company operates in may differ slightly but all will operate under the main elements of:

### Statute Law:

Common law such as duties, negligence, fiduciary etc.,
ASIC Guidelines in Australia,
ASX Listing Rulings Where listing is apropos,
The Company's constitution.

Statute law takes precedence over common law, which takes precedence over other elements such as the company constitution, ASIC guidelines etc. Statute and common law can include State as well as Federal Laws and may differ from state to state. Regulatory bodies that administer and regulate laws and these include the Australian Securities and Investments Commission, or ASIC as it is more commonly known. The Australian Securities Exchange, ASX, the Australian Competition and Consumer Commission, also known as the ACCC, the Federal Privacy Commissioner and the Australian Prudential Regulatory Authority or APRA as they are called.

## Contracts:

Contracts form an important part of a company's business. Every company has contracts of one sort or another, from employment to clients and customers and credits to the leasing of buildings or offices, equipment and, of course, contracts with banks and other financial institutions with respect to funds and, not the least, contracts between the company and shareholders.

A director is not expected to understand all about contracts or even all the contracts a company may have in place. That could amount to hundreds or thousands in the case of a multinational. But a director is expected to have an appreciation of contracts and contract law in general and a director has a responsibility to ensure that there is a system in place to check and monitor all contracts the company undertakes to ensure the company is not disadvantaged by the contracts, that the contracts all fall within the law and guidelines as set out by the various regulatory bodies.

Some contracts will require the attention of the board of directors. Some will not. It will depend on the size of the organisation and the type and scope of the contract and here, delegation is of prime importance.

All companies have certain contracts. The constitution is one prime contract between the company and the shareholders. All directors should be acquainted with the constitution and no new director should take a place on the board without becoming familiar with the company constitution and how it affects the company, the shareholders and other stakeholders in the company.

The director is also responsible to ensure the constitution, as well as any other contracts, is complied with and is not illegally applied to the disadvantage of any stakeholder, such as a shareholder, in the company.

Another important contract is that between the CEO and the company. As the board usually selects the CEO, monitors his or her performance and management, applies a succession plan and even, if the situation warrants it, terminates the CEO's employment. It is important for the board to have a clear understanding of what is expected of the CEO and who the most appropriate candidate is. This should be a formal written agreement, usually professional advice would be sought to assist with this and the terms should include a 'non-competition' clause to ensure, that in the event the CEO leaves, that they do not take anything with them from the company that could cause a disadvantage to the company as a result.

An important contract to be aware of is the appointment of the auditors. This is an appointment the board would recommend to the shareholders. An audit committee is essential to ensure that the financial performance is satisfactory and alerts are in place to note any issues that might arise indicating a change or, poor performance arising. Also, other areas of importance should be audited, such as health and safety, compliance with regulatory statutes and bodies, carbon footprint and so forth. An auditor committee should be able to be objective and apply independence to any audits and reports of audits. This means that no person with any 'conflict of interest' should be serving on an audit committee and in a situation where a conflict of interest is apparent then that member should abstain from the committee as an auditor on that issue.

On this issue of conflicts of interest, this may arise where financial benefits are given to directors or related parties to the company. There are strict limitations on this despite the fact that a contravention does not affect the validity of a contract or transaction entered into.

## Board Approval of Contracts:

The board should have a delegations policy in place to define the types of contract approval required by the board. What contracts should be elevated to board for approval? Usually those types of contracts that come under a larger risk in risk assessment as well as unusual or outstanding issues. Issues that affect the solvency of a company can include: major service contracts, major outsourcing activities, mergers and acquisitions to name but a few.

The smaller the company, the more likely a greater number of contracts will come to the board for review. A risk management policy, or guidelines in handling the risk involved with contracts, is also important, as is being able to assess the risk involved.

The possible and probable, outcomes of a contract, as well as a proper sign-off procedure are all part and parcel of a management policy on the approval of contracts.

## Implications of Contracts:

Any person acting as an officer of the company is assumed to be acting with the authority of the company and the company is, therefore, responsible for that individual's actions and activities on behalf of the company. It is assumed the individual is duly appointed and has the authority to exercise powers bestowed upon them by the company. This assumption can be made even if the individual acts in a fraudulent manner, forges a document or acts in anyway dishonest in any proceedings or their dealings. If a party suspected or knew the officer or individual concerned was acting in a manner contrary to that assumption, they are not in fact entitled to make that assumption.

A director is rarely held personally liable on any contract unless that director knew, or should have known, that the company was insolvent. However, if the company suffered a loss as a result of the contract and entry into the contract was conducted with negligence and a breach of the duty of care required by the director, then the director could be considered liable in that circumstance.

In sec 180(2) relating to the Business Judgement Rule, a director may rely on the judgement of others but he, or she, still has to make an individual assessment of the information regarding the contract and a decision based upon that understanding.

Of course, all important contracts should be drawn up by a legal team, or representative and legal advice should always be sought. Usually a company has standard forms, again constructed by a legal, which can be used for standard applications but any variance to those standard applications would require further legal advice.

Major international contracts are a whole new ball game and the issues of:

What countries laws will apply?

Cultural differences between the countries,

Language and translation issues

All the above will have a bearing on how the contracts are constructed, drawn up and issued. Where public companies are involved, there may be interested parties presenting the possibility of conflicts of interest. The proper rules and statutory laws will need to be observed.

As a standard practice, the higher the risk to the company, the more likely the board will be involved in the decision-making and monitoring process. Such monitoring can involve the following:

- Analysing and discussing the relative costs involved,
- Utilising expert advice with regard to the contract proposed, including receiving it and analysing the advice,
- Analysing management plans for implementation including costs in finance, labour and time Management providing regular updates as to the progress of the implementation,
- Receiving reports on the post as well as prior activities and results,
- Noting any potential lessons for improvement in any future contracts

## Director's Duties in Health and Safety:

Although the wording may vary in each jurisdiction in Australia, the essential meaning and liability of a director is the same when it comes to health and safety and the welfare of employees. Occupational Health and Safety (OHS) is a very important part of a company's due diligence and therefore a director's duties include:

- Ensuring that the workplace is a safe environment, including easy means of access and exit from the work place,
- Ensuring also that any plant or equipment is also safe to work with and poses no risk to health when correctly used,
- The system of working should also be safe and not a danger, or risk, to the employee at any level,
- Ensuring that there is sufficient training and education as well as supervision to ensure the safety of workers and providing adequate facilities for the welfare of employees while working. Examples include toilet facilities, refreshment and first aid facilities.

It is the duty of a director to ensure they have an up-to-date knowledge or information concerning work health and safety measures. A director should also have some understanding of the nature of the operation of the business so they can understand the risks and hazards involved. The risks and hazards of a mining operation are very different to that of retail or service operation. A director should also ensure that appropriate resources are used to identify risks and hazards associated with the workplace of an organisation and also the steps to be taken to minimise or eliminate them. Of course, a director should also be concerned with the reporting of any incidents or hazards or risks that have occurred and be able to respond to them in a timely fashion. Also, to verify the resources used as applicable and appropriate to the risks and hazards that may, or may not, have come up.

It is also important that the company, or organisation, complies with their duties under any current and future

Work Health and Safety Act (or equivalent) and any subsequent related Acts and associated regulations. It should be noted that the provisions are becoming so strict now with regard to health and safety that one can assume, as the trend indicates, that the onus leans now upon the director to show they were not negligent in any matter or breach of the Health and Safety Act rather than on the prosecutor showing cause.

As such, the law in each state applies liabilities to directors for breaches in the OHS laws. In NSW, if a company is found to have breaches in the law, it will be assumed that the directors have also breached the law unless they can satisfy the court that they were not in a position to influence the conduct of the company on this matter or, the director used all due diligence to prevent the breach.

In Tasmania and Queensland the law is essentially the same although the wording is different. The director is still considered culpable and, in fact, even if the company is not found culpable the director(s) may still be considered so.

In Victoria, WA, SA and the North Territory the wording of the relative state acts are different but no less onerous.

A director can be found to be guilty of an offense and this has happened in various cases.

### Director Compliance:

A director has a duty of responsibility to ensure the company is complying with the OHS laws and not simply giving lip service to a set of standards. Responsible officer's duties are considered of prime importance. The fact that the vast majority of prosecutions in NSW under the OHS Act result in a prosecution and conviction brings home the importance to a director of taking their duty of care seriously, such as when the due diligence is 'left to management' without a constant and consistent monitoring of the capabilities and actions of management when discharging their duties in this area.

Raising a defence by a director can be very difficult and is especially made harder where there cannot be shown a heavy emphasis by the director to express a duty of care in ensuring that the OHS Act is not breached. A director or directors, therefore, need to ensure:

- That they are aware of the Act as it relates to the company and its operations
- That the company is complying with the Act
- That management, or whoever is responsible for ensuring that the Act is complied with, is indeed doing so by the use of monitoring and reports
- Those responsible are receiving the appropriate education, training and supervision
- That there is documentation set up that identifies and reports on any and all, potential hazards in the workplace and ensures that the system imposed is implemented
- Ensuring that sufficient resources, including funding, time and space, are allocated to ensure that full OHS measures can be implemented and complied with
- Monitoring and auditing the entire blanket activity of OHS in the company including reporting on the application, implementation and future potential risks.

A director of a board should be well conversant with the OHS requirements of the company and, their position on same should be clearly stated, especially if there is a lack of any of the above bullet points. The director would then make it his duty to bring this to the attention of the board and, if there is no change then his objection should be recorded in the board minutes. Where there is a potential danger of life of violation of the act a director would responsibly report this to the appropriate OHS authorities.

Practicality is an issue that a director can apply in their own defence in some states. This usually amounts to not being able to practically apply the law or, the person had no control over the incident and it was impracticable for the person to make a provision against it. But this is still dependent upon a court and upon prior precedents.

In regard to practicality a court may take into account the severity of the risk involved, the knowledge about the risk or how it could have been removed or mitigated, the ability and suitability of removing the hazard or risk and the cost of same.

Also, if the defendant can show that the circumstances surrounding the incident were not foreseeable then it could be established from that, that it was not practicable to take any measures against that risk.

### Trade Practices Law:

The two main areas of importance when it comes to trade practices law are: Market Conduct rules and Consumer Protection. Both are viewed very seriously and both carry stiff penalties for breaches of the law. They are both geared to outline that competition should not be restricted and that consumers should be treated with fairness.

### Market Conduct Rules:

Market conduct rules are about preventing anti-competitive activities. Competition ensures that there is no monopoly on the goods and services available in a given area and, that no one profits exclusively from an area by reason of a monopoly. Having said that, it is not always economically efficient to have more than one or two providers, or suppliers and so these cases are often taken on a case-by-case basis. The trade practices law would then examine the circumstances and may, under certain circumstances, make provision for less competition if the result is of benefit to the community as a whole. The main conduct rules can be summarised as follows:

## Section 45:

Anti-Competitive agreements, including a competition test,
Price fixing is prohibited,
Exclusionary provision is prohibited.

## Section 46:

Take advantage of substantial market,
Power for prohibited purpose is subject to a special test.

## Section 47:

Exclusive dealing again competition test.

## Section 48:

Resale price maintenance (the practice of a supplier forcing a customer to not sell the Goods below a specified price) is prohibited.

## Section 50:

Mergers are subject to a completion test.

## Consumer Protection:

The penalties for violation of the Consumer Protection law can be seriously heavy. The Competition and Consumer Act 2010 states that: "a corporation shall not, in trade or commerce, engage in conduct that is misleading or deceptive or is likely to mislead or deceive."

Misleading or deceptive announcements to the ASX

Although the above does not apply to financial practices and services is still a similar provision in the Corporations Act of 2001 which reads: "a person shall not, in this jurisdiction, engage in conduct, in relation to a financial product or a financial service that is misleading or deceptive or is likely to mislead or deceive."

This can extend to statement made by companies as well as individuals despite the fact that such statements may not refer to shares, or securities, of the company.

## ACCC

The Australian Competition and Consumer Commission covers three areas:

Consumers,
Business and companies,
Regulated Industries.

According to the ACCC website, "The ACCC promotes competition and fair trade in the market place to benefit consumers, businesses and the community. It also regulates national infrastructure services. Its primary responsibility is to ensure that individuals and businesses comply with the Commonwealth competition, fair trading and consumer protection laws."

Within that scope the ACCC published, in November 2005, the Corporate Trade Practices Compliance Programs.

A 47-page booklet specifically designed for medium to large businesses. The ACCC, in the guide states, "This guide, Corporate trade practices compliance programs, is for medium to large companies implementing, or updating, their trade practices compliance program. It also provides information on how the ACCC administers the obligations entailed by compliance program elements of the undertakings it accepts and why." It indicates that any effective compliance program should have:

Strategic vision: Compliance activities are linked to the company's strategic goals. The method the company will employ to achieve those goals is communicated, as are benchmarks for implementation.

Risk assessment: The company actively identifies its compliance risks and reassesses those risks at regular intervals and, as part of entering into new business areas or activities. Specific compliance risks that may arise within each business unit, or sphere of operations, are considered.

Control Points: Each of the risks is managed at specified control points. Control points are reinforced by establishing behavioural and procedural controls. Procedural mechanisms address and mitigate high-risk areas in a business-operating environment, while the behavioural mechanisms emphasise the company's policies for those risks.

Adequate documentation: Compliance endeavours are adequately documented to ensure they can be substantiated in the event of a breach

Identified positions that are accountable for managing each specific element of the compliance system

Continuous improvement: The company self-evaluates its performance and approach to ensure they are appropriate to its operations

Not all of these guidelines would necessarily be appropriate for all companies, but a company should be tailoring its program along these guidelines.

## Intellectual Property:

An area of concern to any director is intellectual property (IP). Intellectual property is one of the values of a company and the protection of IP should be the concern of the CEO, MD, Chairman and Board of any company or corporation. Apart from the value to a corporation there is the financial accounting to consider with regard to IP. A company's IP can include:

Branding,
Logos,
Copyright,
Confidential information or knowledge,
Trademarks,
Patents and design

Although a director would not be expected to be an expert in IP matters, he should have a basic understanding of the mechanisms relating to IP protection and how they should be implemented.

Policies should be in place, covering the ownership and ethical use of IP, any potential threats to that IP and the nature of any relationship with IP consultants or advisors. Each of these areas is different and so there are differences in the registration and value and in the potential infringements that can occur.

### Copyright:

Copyright is fairly simple and a company, or individual, has a statutory protection on anything that is written, published or not published by them. An infringement would be where the works of another are simply copied, without permission and expressed as one's own where they are not.

It should be noted that the same work created independently would not be an infringement of copyright of one to the other. However, it is likely that substantiation would need to be shown that the creation was independently done and not copied.

Copyright is expressed in material form and does not cover ideas.

### Confidential Material:

Confidential information is somewhat different. Protection is given in common and statutory law and no registration is required for the rights to be maintained. Confidential information can arise where there are contracts or disclosure to third parties for some agreed purpose or some relationship between the parties concerned. This area can cover ideas not materially expressed or in the public domain.

Here, an infringement would be seen as a breach of confidentiality with such information being disclosed to unauthorised parties.

## Trade Marks:

Trade marks issued to distinguish, or identify, a trader's goods and/or services, could be called a stricter version of copyright. Again statutory and common-law rights apply. Usually a trademark infringement is fairly clear-cut and, unlike copyright, independently created trademarks that are of the same, or identical 'sign', can be successfully challenged.

## Patents:

Patents are a different area entirely. A patent is a record of a design, or a 'manner of manufacture', which is new and not previously in the public knowledge and not obvious. There is some ambiguity here as patents of similar items are not always challenged. Patents have statutory protection but also require registration. Like trademarks, infringements can be claimed for similar, or same, even if the similar or same concept has been arrived at independently.

Designs require registration and then they have statutory protection. They must be new and / or distinct (not previously published or used in Australia). A challenge for infringement can be made for a design that is substantially similar on the overall impression or look.

## Strategy in IP:

Having a proper strategy for the overall company's IP management is very important to ensure that the IP is protected and used in a legal and effective way. Such a strategy should also ensure that no infringement of the IP is incurred either by the company or a third party or, that proprietary information is not disclosed without warrant.

The larger the corporation, the more an Audit committee concerns itself with the IP of the corporation. This should include a strategy plan to cover:

- Identification of all IP associated with the business or company.
- Identification of what the company owns and has the right to use and the substantiation to prove this.
- A program to ensure that any registrations connected with the company's IP are maintained and kept up to date. This includes registering any IP that should be registered and is currently not (e.g. client lists and databases),
- Determination of the value of all IP,
- Retention of IP related to marketing or other material produced outside of house,
- IP confidentiality documentation and nondisclosure statements signed by relevant key staff,
- Staff training on the importance of intellectual property and their responsibility in its maintenance and protection.

Although environmental law (EL) varies according to the state, or territory, the company is operating in; it is, nevertheless, an important law which directors should be aware of. Particularly as there can be substantial penalties levied against directors for breaches in the environmental laws.

The environment is considered to include air and water quality, noise, marine environment, site contamination and general protection of the environment.

Here, director due diligence is required to ensure that the company is not engaging in activities prohibited by EL. Directors can be prosecuted for violations and penalties can include heavy fines and even imprisonment.

Defences of due diligence would likely only be acceptable where the director(s) showed they could not have been expected to have had an awareness of the violation.

Environmental audits are probably the best method to ensure a company is complying with environment laws and statutory requirements. Environmental protection agencies will always look to the directors in any violation of applicable laws. Defences of directors and executive officers lie in the establishment that the director, or executive officer, was not able to influence the corporation's conduct in preventing any violation. This means that written documentation, such as board minutes, for example, would be inspected. Also, that a director took reasonable steps to ensure the company was compliant with the law.

If it is established that there was an environmental system in place and, that staff were aware of that system and the system had been effectively applied and was subject to regular reviews and amended as required, then these would be looked upon favourably by the relevant state EPA.

The better the documentation to demonstrate the above, the stronger would be the executive officer, or director's, defence.

## Commercial Transactions:

Commercial transactions may have an environmental aspect that needs to be considered. Commercial transactions include:

Mergers and acquisitions,
Share purchases,
Asset sales (including land, buildings and shares),
Purchasing of land and buildings and,
The leasing of land, buildings and equipment.

Investigation is needed to determine about what is being appropriated, or bought, is environmentally within the law. If it is not, then what costs are involved in clean-up or, what other activities are required to comply with the environmental law.

The same would apply when assets such as land and buildings are sold.

This also applies where a company is acquired. Is that company compliant with environmental issues and if not, what would be required to make it so? Are all legal warranties and indemnities in place, including required insurance and liability protection? These should be included in any contract that involves the sale, or purchase, of any assets (more especially land and buildings).

The director's report should include, where applicable, a report attesting to the company's compliance with environmental issues. If an environmental issue is found to exist, such as a violation of the environment law and this is not recorded in the director's report, such directors could be found to be in breach of the Corporations Act and penalties can include heavy fines and even imprisonment.

## Climate Change and Carbon Footprint:

The final form of legislation on climate change, carbon footprint and greenhouse gas emissions, is yet to be finalised at the time of writing. However, Directors should be aware of the possible implications such legislation may have on the company and what activities might be appropriate to comply with them. These may include looking at future risk, sustainability of the business model and reporting obligations.

## Anti-Discrimination Laws:

The principle types of discrimination include: race, skin colour, gender, sexual orientation, disability, age, religion or political beliefs. Anti-Discriminatory laws are such that it is not enough for an organisation to have anti-discriminatory policies in place, but it must be shown that the employees are fully aware of them and, that the policies can be seen to have been enforced. This includes indirect discrimination as well as direct. Sometimes a balance needs to be set with OHS requirements, as there can be a conflict in this area. An example might be, restricting a person from doing overtime when on light duties after medical treatment or working alone in an office.

## Privacy:

Privacy covers more areas than one might initially consider. As well as privacy of information about an individual, there is also privacy about customers of a company. There are also such issues as staff morale, avoiding potential legal costs and penalties and corporate moral and social responsibility.

Many instances of privacy being violated through exposure of confidential information via the internet, for example, have shown that a company can suffer big risks to their reputation and brand, as well as potential legal action from those who allege a privacy violation has led to the loss of valuable and vital information.

The Privacy Act of 1988 sets out ten basic privacy principles (National Privacy Principles—[NPPs]), which include how data and private information is collected, stored and secured. It also covers areas such as transferring information outside of Australia, as well as how to handle sensitive information. A board needs to be cognisant of the importance and need for privacy and have in place a Privacy and Confidentiality policy that is used by all staff within their organisation.

It should be noted that the NPPs apply to all businesses with an annual turnover of over three million dollars, as well as all health service providers. Those exempts are businesses with a turnover of less than three million dollars, unless they are related to a business with more than three million turnover or, provide health services and keep health records or, are contracted to provide a service on a commonwealth contract or, provide others with benefits of a health nature.

The Privacy Act includes consumer credit reporting which ensures that information obtained is only applied for assessing credit applications. It is up to the board to ensure that appropriate training in privacy is provided and that there is at least one person on the board who is an expert in privacy matters. There should be a person, or committee, who is accountable for the company's privacy compliance.

Compliance to the privacy policy should be a part of management's performance evaluation and periodic assessments (including audits) should be done to ensure compliance is being adhered to, with reports going to the board on the matter.

Lastly, the board should be able to ask the right questions of management about existing privacy practices in the organisation.

## Other Major Legal Issues for Directors:

Over the past few years, it has become increasingly apparent that boards need to pay more attention to tax issues. This is not to say they should become tax experts for the company but rather, they do have a responsibility to ensure that a framework for the management of tax is in place, that the company is within the legal boundaries of tax compliance and that the company meets its tax obligations and has a system in place to manage those obligations.

Issues that may come before a board in this area include:

Is the company legally tax compliant? Is it possible the ATO will take a different viewpoint of the tax liabilities of the company to those of the company's tax advisors? If so what would the consequences be? Is it likely to go to court? If there was a dispute, would the ATO agree to a settlement? Would such activity increase or decrease the future potential tax liability? What are the risks and benefits in asking for a private ruling on certain tax issues?

How satisfied is the board with the current taxation advice being given?

If the ATO considers a company is failing to meet its tax obligations and issues a director's penalty notice, the directors must comply with the taxation obligations or, make an agreement with the ATO or, if no other alternative, appoint an administrator or, begin to wind-up the company. Failing to do any of the above, the directors can become personally liable for the debt and as a company's tax can be vastly more than personal tax, this can be well outside the scope of the directors' ability to pay. Mitigating circumstances might include where a director can substantiate he /she did not participate in the management of the company at the time the tax obligation was incurred or, that they took all reasonable steps to ensure the company meet its tax obligations.

A new director to a board has 14 days to ensure the company is meeting its tax obligations or, be included in any penalty liability. It behoves, therefore, any new director to ensure that the company he / she is proposing to be on the board of, has met all its prior tax obligations.

### E-Businesses:

Many business operate through the internet via websites, blogs etc. Potential legal issues can arise where there is a lack of security concerning data, availability and usage of the website. One of the more important criteria is ensuring the company website remains up to date. The board have a responsibility to ensure that a management system is in place to:

Monitor and keep updated the internet activities of the company,

Ensure compliance with regulatory issues, such as trade description and up-to-date price lists,

Monitor the communication lines to ensure spam and other unwanted communications are not issued by the company website in contravention of applicable regulations, including overseas regulations,

All websites should also have the relevant disclaimers and terms of service,

Privacy policies should be clearly stated particularly with the changes in privacy policies in Europe now filtering through to other countries, including Australia.

### Outsourcing:

Outsourcing of work activities need to be well managed to ensure that contractual obligations are fully met. Where a company outsources large contracts the board would need to consider that:

A business case study is developed if required to determine the economic feasibility for outsourcing the activity or work or material supply,

A proper tender process is in place,

Due diligence of the selected contractor has been done,

The board has established the suitability of the management process or, if undertaking the study themselves, approved the agreements put in place. Having a monitoring system in place on outsourcing agreements including the compliance with statutory and common law regulations and reviewing the production and results of the agreements in place.

## Anti-Money Laundering:

This area aligns closely with the Privacy Act, in that under the Anti-money Laundering and Counterterrorism Act one needs to collect identifiable information about individuals, usually customers and clients and yet this information needs to remain confidential and is subject to disclosure to reverent authorities under the Act when the authorities deem the disclosure is warranted. It mainly applies to providers that supply financial, bullion or gambling services and includes:

- Reporting customer or client identities
- Reporting any suspicious behaviours
- Reporting transactions over a specific value
- Having and maintaining an active anti-money laundering and counter-terrorism financial program and
- Keeping accurate and appropriate records.

It would be the board's responsibility to ensure such policies and systems are in place and that the staff is aware of them and use them.

It is worth noting here that such policies should be made known in privacy statements issued by the company such as on websites and in written material.

## Conclusion:

Broadly, then, the Board of Directors of any company, large or small, has a duty to ensure that the organisation conforms with the legal requirements of the countries in which it operates

# Corporate Responsibility

Corporate responsibility can be taken too lightly. For many boards, corporate responsibility extends to just the company shareholders and overlooks the broader picture. How are board's decisions impacting on the broader scale? Under common law in the western world, board members have a responsibility:

To act honestly,

Exercise reasonable care and skill and

Understand their fiduciary duties whilst performing their necessary tasks

The board's responsibility is one of stewardship and trusteeship on behalf of stakeholders and is ultimately accountable for all organisation matters. This responsibility includes:

Liaising with key stakeholders such as management of the company, staff and clients to inform them of achievements and acknowledging contributions towards determining strategic goals and direction,

Appointing Chief Executive Officer (CEO), providing guidance and advice as required and setting targets in order to evaluate the performance of and reward as appropriate, the CEO,

Putting into place appropriate corporate governance structures including standards of ethical behaviour promoting a culture of corporate and social responsibility,

Monitoring the CEO and the company's compliance with the relevant federal, state and local legislation and bylaws and with the organisation's own internal policies,

Monitoring the company's strategic business plans and direction and their performance including the annual budget outcomes,

Setting the company's strategic direction,

Reporting to all stakeholders at the Annual General Meeting (AGM),

Making sure a firm policy framework for governing the organisation is in effect and from which all operational policies and actions may be developed,

Having in place a Risk Management Plan to assessing all potential risks facing the organisation and monitoring its compliance.

# The Board's Code of Conduct

All boards have not just a legal, but a moral responsibility to manage their organisation in the best interests of the community it serves. Board members should apply professional ethical behaviour at all times not just in their responsibilities to the organisation but in their professional relationships with each other and their professional service to the community.

A code of conduct provides clarity about the expected behaviours of board and this should be one area of interest to you should you be considering joining a board. Is their Code of conduct compatible with your own?

A good Code of Conduct for a director should demonstrate, as a minimum, the following:

- Not honesty alone, but the punctilio (1. A fine point of etiquette 2. Precise observance of formalities) of an honour the most sensitive should be the standard of behaviour for directors with regard to their relations with other board members, stakeholders and members of their public
- The application of appropriate codes of conduct is the expected standard of professionalism for a Director Performance of the duties of his or her office impartially, uninfluenced by fear or favour
- Make no improper use of information acquired as a result of his or her position as a board member to gain, indirectly or directly, an advantage for himself

or herself or for any other person or to cause detriment in any way
- Not allowing the personal interests or the interests of any associated persons, such as family, friends etc. or other favourable interests to conflict with the interests of the company
- Do not engage in conduct likely to bring discredit upon the organisation either publicly or privately
- Be fully cognisant with the roles, responsibilities and reporting relationships of the board and professional staff
- Not individually instruct the Chief Executive Officer on matters relating to operational issues but issue instructions from the board as a whole
- Attend all board meetings. Where attendance is not possible members will submit an apology. If absence is likely to extend for several consecutive meetings, members will obtain leave of absence
- At board meetings following the protocol of board meeting such as recognising the authority of the Chair, listening to and respecting the opinions of fellow colleagues and debating issues in a non-threatening, cooperative manner at all times
- Being fully prepared for meetings by preparing for meetings by having complete reports and able to read and consider papers circulated prior to and during a board meeting
- Express concerns to the Chairperson or other relevant authority about decisions or actions contrary to the board's public duty
- Maintain confidentiality and do not divulge information deemed confidential or sensitive. If members are uncertain about the confidentiality of certain matters, they should seek direction from the Chairperson. This also includes avoiding discussing board business in public places where there is a likelihood of being overheard

- Have an obligation to be independent in judgement and actions and to take reasonable steps to be satisfied as to the soundness of all decisions of the board
- Ensure that the organisation's assets are protected via a suitable risk management strategy
- Not accepting, asking for or demanding any fee, gratuity, gift, remuneration or other recompense in connection with their official duties outside the scope of their entitlements as a board member unless authorised by the chairperson
- Have an obligation to comply with the spirit, as well as the letter of the law and with the principles of this code.

# Corporate Governance

Governance is a word that is bandied around a lot these days, particularly when it comes to board directors and their responsibilities. One the one hand, we have board directors insisting on the scope they require to apply good governance and on the other we have governmental institutions insisting that boundaries are needed to control the activities of board directors.

Of course, any function requires some boundaries as well as freedoms. But where do these boundaries and freedoms extend and who sets out the role of directors in boards. Further, how far should government go in imposing boundaries for corporate governance? And at what point is the responsibility of directors overshadowed by too much legislation with regard to director's functions and range of activities?

Let's look at some basics to help to understand this issue.

## Governance:

Governance has been around since the dawn of civilisation. We see it in history with governments going back to the Roman Empire and again further back in the Chinese Courts many thousands of years ago. Governing the country or the land, setting up laws and basically stating the freedoms and barriers under which the country would operate.

The term governance refers to the activity of exercising and directing an influence over the decision making and how these decisions are put into effect. This comes from governing, to direct and control the actions, affairs, policies, functions, etc., of (a political unit, organisation, nation, etc.); rule. It also means to be a predominant influence on (something): to decide or determine. The word comes from the old French word, *gouverner*, originating from the Latin *gubern* meaning to steer and possibly from the early Greek *kubernan*.

Probably the Latin derivation is the most accurate for our purposes.

To steer and guide an organisation in the desired direction.

Corporate Governance encompasses a wide range of structures designed to push forward the goals or mission statement of the organisation. This would include accountability, responsibility, economic efficiency, strategic aptitude among others. In governance various stakeholders need to be addressed, such as stockholders, the well-being of the organisation, its employees, officers and management and external groups such as consumer groups, green issues, addressed neighbourhoods, the community as a whole and the environment etc.

So governance is the system of guiding and steering the group, organisation, company or department towards a stated objective by those selected to apply the governance. It includes, making sure that the organisation conforms to the laws and statutes of the country in which it operates. That it operates in an efficient and profitable manner but not to the detriment of its resources, including manpower, its stakeholders, such as investors and shareholders, creditors, consumers, etc. That it works to achieve the goals set out by the goal setter, often the founder of the organisation but can include the board of directors these days. It is the system used to direct and control companies.

This includes ensuring economic efficiency, profitability, good relations with stakeholders, such as shareholders, creditors and indeed management and employees.

The board of directors of any organisation are concerned with the forward progress of the organisation towards the stated goals or mission statements. The larger the organisation the more broad is likely to be their strategy. Also the more 'extended' functions such as committees to ensure regulatory compliance, financial, health and safety, remuneration and so forth, would be set up and report to the board.

The role of governance includes:

1. **Communication:** Being effective in the communication with the CEO, management and stakeholders ensuring that all are appraised
2. **Strategy:** Setting out the business objectives and strategy required to meet them. This includes setting a strategic corporate plan to attain the vision for the future for the organisation. This a broad long-range plan and different to the annual business plan that would outline the objectives for the coming year but which should also integrate with the long-range planning set out
3. **Responsibility:** Accepting responsibility for the stewardship of the organisation and for ensuring that the organisation is performing within the regulatory framework for companies and directors. Ensuring that the organisation is financially viable and acting in a financially responsible manner
4. **Business Planning:** Thinking through and documenting the best considered strategic direction and how to implement it

## Analysing Environmental Factors:

### Identifying the current objectives:

Developing and ensuring implemented appropriate policies that forward the strategic plan for the organisation

**Performance monitoring and reporting:**
Receive reports on various areas such as financial, environmental impact, risk management, for larger organisations, remuneration reports, reports on director's proficiency etc.

**Stewardship:**
Provide leadership and monitoring for new directors although this tends to be more the responsibility of the chair (Chairman of the board)

A word on the Chairman of a Board (Chair). He or she has a broad range of duties, in addition to being a board member, that include:

Ensuring that all board members can express their views and that they all participate in the decision-making process,

Ensuring that the board has available all the relevant policy documents to do their duty,

Setting the board agenda ensuring that all appropriate items are included

## Running the Board Meetings:

And that, as a first duty, any conflicts of interest or duty is raise at the beginning of the meeting in the event any board members needs to recluse him or herself from the meeting in accordance with board policy.

The chair has a role to ensure a balance is maintained to ensure that all board members have a fair opportunity to ask questions and express their views.

Directors have a duty to follow a code of conduct which includes, acting with honesty and integrity.

Being open and transparent in their dealings.

Using power responsibly and not placing them in a position that would involve a conflict of interest.

## Directors Need To:

Act in good faith in the best interests of the company, demonstrating accountability for their actions and accepting responsibility for their decisions. Act fairly and impartially avoiding any bias, discrimination, caprice or self-interest. They should demonstrate respect for others, acting in a professional and courteous manner. This also includes avoiding any conflict of interest (more on conflict of interest below). This is particularly important where a board member serves on more than one board.

Information obtained or given should be used appropriately and applied to the proper purpose to which it relates and kept confidential.

The board member should apply his position appropriately. This means to not use the position as a director to seek an undue or unfair advantage for oneself, one's family members, 'mates' or associates. This includes ensuring that he or she declines gifts or favours that may be construed as a bribe or kickback and cast doubt on their application of independent judgement as a director of the company. It also means not participating in insider information activities.

It is vitally important that a director has a good grasp and understanding of the financial reports of a company. This means acting in a financially responsible manner. Being able to read and understand financial reports, audit reports and other financial material that comes before the board is a prime activity of a company director.

A director has to have a good grasp of strategy and how it should be applied to the decisions of the board. Strategy should always be applied to the best interests of the relevant stakeholders, such as shareholders for example. The Board of Directors is there to direct the progress and expansion of the company through planning, deciding policy and direction.

A board member must integrate smoothly with the board as a whole offering his or her thoughts, while also allowing others on the board to voice theirs.

## Exercising Due Care:

Doing ones due diligence to gather all relevant information,

Making all efforts to understand the financial, strategic and other make reasonable enquiries: understand the financial, strategic and other implications of decisions,

Being punctilious* with regard to honesty and the expected standard of behaviour including acting honestly, in good faith and with the best interests of the company. Integrity plays a big part in this.

Being compliant with the various acts and regulations as pertains to corporate governance and responsibility,

Any and all information that comes across the board or the director in his or her capacity as a board member should remain confidential and the board member is responsible for ensuring the security of information in their keeping. The only exception being information which one is legally obliged to provide to authorised bodies by law.

## Conflict Of Interest:

Conflict of interest is sufficiently important enough to warrant further discussion.

A board member has the responsibility to ensure there is no conflict of interest by him in his capacity as a board member. If any conflict of interest arises or becomes evident, then it would need to be managed in accordance with the policy of the company. Such a conflict might be of a personal nature or interest (directly or indirectly—such as a spouse having an interest financial or otherwise that might be considered in conflict with one's role on a board) or from a duty one is performing with another organisation, such as a board role for another company, for example.

A conflict of interest can be real or potential or even just perceived. In all cases the board member has the duty to speak up whether the conflict is their own or that of another board member to ensure the conflict is identified and managed so as to not affect the performance of the board members duty. Staff should also be empowered and supported to speak up about any conflicts.

Being a board member is a trusted responsibility and not to be taken lightly. It is also an extremely rewarding endeavour that gives great satisfaction as a leader in society.

## Integrity and its Part in Corporate Governance:

Here we take an extended look at issues relating more to qualities relating to an individual and perspective board member than the board as a whole. The board member has duties and responsibilities that extend further than just 'being a board member'. Personal integrity and responsibility play a major part in a board member's make up.

As a board member operates in an unstructured environment as distinct to an executive arena, a more disciplined and responsible role is required of a director than of an executive in a management role. An executive arena is more structured and the executive has direct accountability to senior management and senior management to the CEO or Executive Director and he or she to the board. In a board position, although accountability and responsibility is shared with the other members of the board, the director still has a more autonomous role in many respects and consequently needs a higher level of integrity, discipline and responsibility to operate effectively.

## Integrity and Responsibility:

Integrity and responsibility pay a vital role in the arsenal of the Non-Executive Director (NED). The dictionary definition of integrity includes:

"Adherence to moral and ethical principles; soundness of moral character; honesty. The state of being whole, entire, or undiminished. A sound unimpaired or perfect condition."

Its origin is c.1450, "wholeness, perfect condition," from O.Fr. *integritè*, from L. *integritatem* (nom. *integritas*) "soundness, wholeness," from integer "whole" (see integer). Sense of "uncorrupted virtue" from 1548.

As has been mentioned before but bears repeating, Thomas McCauley defined integrity well when he said:

"The measure of a man's real character is what he would do if he would never be found out."

Integrity could be said to be the composite of a triangle, one corner of which is honesty, another responsibility and the third, discipline. It takes honesty, responsibility and discipline in order to have integrity. If any one of these fails then the integrity as a whole falls to the ground. To restore integrity it is only required to ensure all three corners of the triangle are upheld with emphasis on the first, honesty. However, the integrity of an individual is also a reflection of the ethics and mores of the individual. What is acceptable ethics for one person may not be acceptable for another. This is why it is important for the Non-Executive Director (NED) to be a close fit with the board from his point of view as well as the boards.

There are agreed upon rules of ethics and engagement in a board with which one is expected to adhere to as a NED. When one joins a board one is essentially agreeing with the moral precepts and ethical standards of that board. In addition, ethics is not a case of black or white. There can be infinite shades of grey and these shades of grade are where integrity becomes most important for an NED.

### Full Responsibility:

"You are responsible for everything that happens to you."
– Eleanor Roosevelt

There are many definitions for responsibility but a good one for our purposes is:

"Having a capacity for moral decisions and therefore accountable; capable of rational thought or action and chargeable with being the author, cause, or occasion of something."

It derives from Latin *responsum*, noun use of neuter past participle of *respondere* to respond; replacing Middle English *respounse* < Middle French *respons*.

Responsibility could almost be regarded as an ability and like many abilities the more it is practiced the better one gets at it. By the same token the less one practices applying responsibility the less capable one becomes. Responsibility is an activity. Not passivity. Even if one was not initially responsible for an activity, the moment one joins a board one immediately shares responsibility for the decisions and actions of the board and one can assume responsibility for it and thereby assume a measure of control over that activity and effect a change.

Further. The circumstances or economic climate do not matter. Assuming full responsibility means not accepting any excuses or justifications or reassigning responsibility outside of one's area of influence. It means, come what may, one is ultimately responsible for the board's decisions and activities as a whole as well as for one's individual decisions. Taking full responsibility places the director into a more causative role and extends his or her ability to take action.

## Barriers and Freedoms:

While it is important to have a regulatory field within which to operate, too much regulation can be just as bad as too little. A highly regulated field confines the board and tends to promote hesitancy in the decision making process. Should we act or not? Is there a regulation that will impact on our decision in a particular matter and what are the consequences of this? Where a board is more concerned with consequences rather than results, the board will lack direction and leadership and even proper and due governance since they will not be making good decisions on behalf of the shareholder and the good of the company but simply in order to conform to regulations only.

On the other hand, having little or no regulation means that the board can run wild and cause potential harm to the company through an unrestricted decision making process. So a balance needs to be struck that enables effective governance within the scope of the regulatory structure to which the board must adhere while observing the requirements of that regulatory position.

Responsibility is also proportional to the amount of regulation that exists. The more regulation imposed, the less responsibility required and in some cases that is not a good thing as ones area of responsibility and accountability is reduced across the board (no pun intended). No regulation would mean that total responsibility would be required by the board and board member.

The scope of a director's influence within and, indeed, outside of the board, means that with freedom to act comes honesty, discipline and responsibility.

## Personal Conflicts of Interest:

As well as the conflicts of interest that is generally understood may exist in a board position, they can also be personal conflicts of interest that may not always be apparent for the individual board member. An obvious example, of course, is a board member who is a vegetarian serving on a meat marketing board but less obviously is a board member with one set of ethics values serving on a board that has a different set of ethical values. Such as with religious or philosophical views at variance with the board's values and philosophy.

Even less obvious is serving with other directors with different ethical or moral standards and with which one can be hard put to reconcile. All of this is part and parcel of ensuring a good 'fit' with the board. From the point of view of the director also, is the board a good fit for him or her?

The results of a board in which all members are conscious of the importance of their integrity and how this is reflected in board decisions can be quite marked.

Being a board member is a trusted responsibility and not to be taken lightly. It is also an extremely rewarding endeavour that gives great satisfaction as a leader in society.

A board that has the highest standards of integrity will make correspondingly optimum decisions for the benefit of the company, its shareholders and stakeholders and will serve the company well. Remember, the board member is not just a captain of industry but is also a servant by virtue of service to the board and the company. He or she is there to give their very best service to the company and most board members do just that.

## The Customer:

As we have seen recently in Australia with the Royal Banking Commission, the customer or client of the company can get left by the way side or, indeed, taken financial advantage of in the interest of the board, the company and, disturbingly, on behalf of the shareholders. This is where it is prudent to inspect the purposes and motives of the board. It is also where the integrity as outlined previously should be employed.

The purpose and duties of the board should not include any practice that violates the integrity of the board either collectively or on an individual basis either knowingly or unknowingly. That may seem rather harsh but ignorance is no excuse for failing in ones duties as a board member. All the previous precepts outlined apply including honesty and maintaining a strict ethical standpoint. One should not, for example, as a board member, be encouraged and or expected to violate the community standards to which the board and the corporate body has agreed to. This would:

Incur a conflict of interest, where one's interest of being successful, for example, is at the expense of the client or customer of the company,

Potentially incur further regulation of the board's decision-making process and activities,

Violate one's integrity and accountability for making a moral decision,

Violating one's trust with the shareholders and the public,

The above may produce a lack of trust in the company by the public, the shareholders and even one's peers resulting in a contraction of the company including a drop in the share price and perceived value of the company.

Indeed, we have seen this exact scenario with AMP in Australia (AMP is a financial services company in Australia and New Zealand providing superannuation and investment products, insurance, financial advice and banking products including home loans and savings accounts) where it was found that the board had violated many of the principles found in this book and, as a result, suffered a severe drop in their share price to less than a third of their original price. They also suffered the loss of directors and over 60% of shareholders voting against the board's remuneration and with the revelation of severe misconduct which may still result in criminal proceedings against board members. Importantly the loss of credibility of the company was extreme in the least and it will take many years for the company recover.

Not only AMP but other financial institutions, including the four big banks in Australia, have been exposed for financial malpractice and unconscionable behaviours on a grand scale which has resulted in at least one CEO (Commonwealth Bank) stood down and others may follow. These activities have also, predictably, resulted in a call for more strenuous regulation.

In view of the examples above it behoves every board to act with integrity, honesty and discipline to ensure they forward the purposes and goals of the company in a manner consistent with the principles laid down in this book.

Doing so will go a long way to ensuring trust by the community and the clients and customers who, after all, are those which provide the company with the business and the value it aspires to have.

## Joining a Board:

If you are looking at joining a board, there are a number of factors to take into consideration. These form part of the due diligence one should perform before one considers joining a particular board.

As one is likely to be taking on the responsibilities of the board, for the past as well as present and future strategies and decisions, it behoves one to pay particular attention to the board's structure and operating basis.

Some questions one can ask include:

Is this an active board focusing on performing its fiduciary and compliance requirements or does it take a passive, wait and see approach?

How does the chairman run the board? Does he take a dictatorial or a consultative approach? Does he act as a mentor to the board members and is he willing to guide the board members on course as a captain would guide a ship? Is he truly a captain of industry?

How do the board members relate to each other? Is there a compatible relationship and is it a relationship that one can integrate with?

Does the board have a mission statement and goal(s) for the company and are these in alignment with one's own?

Is there a well thought out strategic planning for the company direction to achieve this mission statement and goals?

Does this include the risks, such as market shift for example and the ability to execute the laid-out strategy?

How does the board obtain the information they need to make decisions?

Are there committees that serve to provide this information?

Are any of the board members on those committees?

Would you be expected to serve on a committee, say an audit committee for example? Would that be a good fit for you?

Does the board meet with the customers or clients of the company to obtain information that is not 'sanitised'?

What is the relationship of the board with management? Is it a cooperative relationship or are their strains?

Do discussions occur regularly and is there a good interface between the audit and other committees and the board?

What is the attitude of the board to shareholders? Is there a good and effective relationship between the board and the shareholders? Are the shareholders happy with the board's strategy and decisions?

How does the board handle conflicts between them and management and or shareholders?

Is there an orientation program or guidance to bring new board members up to speed or are they just thrown in to fend for themselves?

What steps have been taken to put in place a crises management program in the eventuality it will be needed?

Check over the financials. One should have access to the past five year's financial balance sheet and cash flows. Have there been any difficulties? How much debt does the company carry and what provisions are in place to manage that debt. How does the board keep alert to financial risk and any red alerts that may arise?

How does the board handle legal matters? Are they abreast of any potential legal threats or litigation that can impact on the well-being of the company? Are the directors Insured? This is most important. Also, if an impending legal issue arises, would the insurance company pay for legal fees for the director or directors up front?

Looking and answering the above will give one a good feeling for the board and if it is going to be a good fit.

Which leads us to the question of remuneration? Is the remuneration offered on par with the responsibilities that will be undertaken? What is included in the package? Is it clearly defined or rather vague?

What can you bring to the board?

It is important to understand what you are bringing to a board and that the board can see, understand and appreciate the skills, knowledge and experience you are bring to the table. Why should the board select you out of what may be dozens of potential candidates?

What contribution will you make to the board and the company as a whole?

The above questions asked and answered satisfactorily, will give one a good insight and understanding of a board and how one would fit in and if indeed it is the right board for you and you are right for the board.

# Basics of Business Networking

Business networking is a system or communications method of creating opportunities to share knowledge between professional people. The dictionary defines networking as:

A supportive system of sharing information and services among individuals and groups having a common interest and the action of interacting with others to exchange information and develop professional or social contacts

But of course it is much more than that. Business networking can be seen as a marketing tool or method to create new opportunities, share knowledge and find new ideas through contacts of like-minded business people. One can share information by utilising a business network of a group of business owners and/or employees with common interests and goals.

Business networking is a relatively low cost opportunity to develop contacts, based on referrals and introductions.

This would be either face-to-face at meetings and gatherings and can even be through other contact methods such as phone, email and, increasingly, social and business networking websites.

Business networking also offers a pathway to decision-makers which one might otherwise not be able to contact as it can be an opportunity to gain a personal introduction to that decision maker one has been trying to reach for some time.

Business networking, also called relationship marketing in some circles, expands your area of influence and possibilities of business opportunities.

Business networking is an important and very essential tool in a business person's arsenal these days.

Business networking is about getting one self-known, getting ones values, integrity and passion known as well as developing ones skills and getting the right strategies in place to enhance ones business.

Business networking is an essential tool these days in the competitive market place.

There are a number of steps one can take for successful business networking.

## Step One: What Is The Purpose?

Why do you want to network? For most businesses the purpose is always going to be driven by the business need to expand. This would include expanding the client base, increase brand awareness, expanding the target market and, ultimately, increasing company sales. The purpose or purposes should be very clearly defined.

## Step Two: Have a Clear Goal or Goals

The goal is what you would like to achieve and so this, also, should be very clearly stated. You may have many goals when it comes to business networking. To work out these goals, you might need to identify the person and type of industry you wish to make contact with. What networks will you use, business, personal or both? What do you want to achieve from each contact and relationship you create? What sort of questions or network strategies should you employ to achieve your goals?

What is the overall goal you want to achieve? What would you like to achieve from each business network contact you make?

## Step Three: Be Prepared

When you meet people at social events and gatherings, it is a good idea to have a number of openings you can choose from to start a conversation with someone. It is not professional to fumble and have to be hesitant and not sure what to say. Usually three or four opening lines you can readily call upon, is sufficient for most new contacts.

"What drew you here today?"

"What do you enjoy most about your profession?"

"What did you like about the presentation?"

"Your company sounds very interesting; perhaps you can tell me something about it?"

Above are some examples. The more you have up your sleeve, the wider range of contacts you will be able to approach.

If you come up with a situation and are not sure how to start you could start by asking questions about the person, company or why they are there. Most people love talking about themselves and this is usually a great conversation starter.

If you ask someone enough about themselves, eventually they are going to start asking you about you. So then you need to have an agenda.

## Step Four: Have an Agenda

A good idea is to have two lists. A 'get' list and a 'give' list. The 'get' list is a list of who you want to meet. Who you want to do business with, seek work opportunities or business opportunities with or even just learn more about. The 'give' list is more about what you can give to others in terms of expertise, information of value to others and so forth. If in doubt it is a good idea to start with the 'give' list. What can you give the person in front of you that they might find valuable?

## Step Five: Active Listening

Once you've asked your opening question, that is the key time to listen to the person's answer. Allow the speaker to elaborate without rushing to jump in. Make sure you understand what the person is saying. Ask for clarification, if needed. Ask yourself, "What does this person need? What can I give to this person that would be of value to them?" And "Do I have any knowledge or contacts that can help them?" Avoid glancing around the room to see who else you can talk to. Keep your attention on the person in front of you. Let them know you are interested in them and what they have to say. Be genuine about it.

## Step Six: Find Some Common Ground or Areas of Agreement

Once you have heard from the person, you should be able to find some common ground, some areas of agreement that you can expand on. That is the area you would share your experiences and thoughts on. Let the conversation take you naturally to where you are both comfortable. Avoid over engineering a conversation.

This is not making a sale according to a script. It is developing relationships that may one day result in a mutual benefit to both parties.

## Step Seven: Do Not be Afraid to Ask for Help

People love helping others. Do not be afraid to ask. Suggest mutual ways in which you can help each other. This is what networking is about. Remember the other person is there for exactly the same reason you are. To develop relationships that may contribute to the expansion of their business. At some point they will EXPECT you to ask for help just as they may do with you.

## Step Eight: Following Through

If you want to continuing the relationship you have been developing, then a follow through will be in order. Suggesting a further meeting or:

"I can send that material over to you if you like, what's your email address?"

"Let's set up a time we can go over this in more detail, perhaps over lunch?"

The other person may even make a suggestion for a follow through. This is a time when you can develop a relationship even more. Keep in mind that although there may not necessarily be any immediate advantage to you in doing this there can be long-term advantages. Possibly some business, further down the track.

Your new relationship might suggest you to someone else who is interested in your services; this is all part of networking. Creating a network of relationships that are living and to which, not only can you get something out of, but that you can contribute to also and so build a solid relationship base.

### Social Networking:

Networking strategies include using the social networks to build relationships. There are many networks and tools one can use to share ideas, media and information with others. Such networks, of course, include Facebook, LinkedIn, MySpace, Twitter and a plethora of others. These networks give one the opportunity to strut one's stuff, as it were. Create a personal profile, form up or join groups and interact with one's peers. This is just the ground work however and the basis to develop and form relationships with others that enhance your brand or company's reputation through the interaction with others.

In addition, the advertising on such sites can be very powerful and worthwhile checking out.

The social networking strategy you use will depend largely on the type of company you have, your resources in terms of time and finance, how you represent your company, your marketing strategy and what you have to offer to others that they may be interested in.

Your social networking strategy could be as simple as maintaining a blog and interacting with a reader base through comments and replies to discuss articles and ideas. Or it could be simply maintaining a LinkedIn page for your business. It might be a planned campaign using all the social media available including advertising to back up and increase your presence on line. Importantly, whichever strategy your business employs, it is vitally important that is conducted professionally and managed in the same professional manner any other aspect of your wider communications strategy would be.

## Social Media Contacts:

It has been said that we are only a few steps from knowing basically everyone on the planet and everyone you know and do not know is connected to you in some way.

"Six degrees of separation is the theory that everyone and everything is six or fewer steps away, by way of introduction, from any other person in the world, so that a chain of 'a friend of a friend' statements can be made to connect any two people in a maximum of six steps. It was originally set out by Frigyes Karinthy and popularised by a play written by John Guare."

This is the basic theory behind all social and business networking. And with the various networks now available throughout the world this is indeed very possible. The importance of this emphasises the fact that one cannot achieve anything without the cooperation of others, whether, clients, customers, employees, employers, friends, acquaintances or even, in some cases, competitors. Emphasizing that point is the fact that it usually takes a team to achieve a goal or purpose and having a wide and solid network of contacts will make a big difference to your overall expansion. But networking is not just the province of the social networks through a computer. There are associations and clubs one can join. Meeting people in daily life, such as in a bar or restaurant, a plane or social gathering, are all potential situations to meeting new people. It should also be mentioned that attending networking events will give you a greater opportunity to practice your skills in a controlled environment, where networking is encouraged and expected.

I know one person who built a business simply by sitting in chairs in a shopping mall and talking to people. His target was to talk to ten people a day about his business. He said that only one person in ten showed any interest and few of those took it any further. But he persevered and continued to talk to ten people a day come what may. He now has, after about two years, business worth many thousands and with hundreds of people working for him in a multi-level marketing business selling one product only.

The broader the diversity and source of your networks, the wider the range of different types of contacts you will make. This will help to improve the development of contacts and relationships that can help you in a number of ways and not just providing a single source of benefit for your business.

Of course, the more contacts you make, the more you will enjoy the benefits of networking such as:

Word-of-mouth advertising,

An improvement in your business performance and products,

A boost in your reputation,

Establishment of staff exchanges,

The help and assistance available through professional networking allows you to meet with other business owners that have faced similar problems in the past,

And, importantly, reliable contacts. Professional networking allows you to establish relationships with businesses that could be helpful when you need a particular service in the future

## Professional Networks and Associations:

Professional networks and associations which, have a diversity of people, are likely the best rather than all the same profession. If one is an accountant, for example, although there are advantages to being a member of an accounting association, it is hardly the place to develop new relationships with others with a few to enhancing ones business. Better a Chamber of Commerce or a group that has a diversity of other professions that opens the door to further opportunities.

Researching the options available is a first step. Evaluating which associations or groups, forums etc., align more closely with your goals and objectives in networking would be another step. Attending various meetings and conferences on a subject enables you to focus on changes and advances within that industry and offers the chance to meet others and establish more professional networks.

Social networks include, Facebook, LinkedIn, Meettheboss, PartnerUp, Qapacity, Ryze and XING. There are also many others and all provide the opportunity of staying in contact with people you have already developed or know as well as extending your reach to other contacts.

Networking groups are designed specifically with networking in mind for its members. One goes to a networking group meeting with a bunch of cards in hand specifically to meet more people. Others are doing the same there of course and many relationships and struck up at such meetings. Many associations will hold network meetings. The Australian Institute of Company Directors for example, where one can meet other professionals from a variety of industries and professions.

Professional associations can raise the profile of a particular profession or industry group and provide continuing professional education for their members. The larger associations, such as the Institute of Chartered Accountants in Australia, have their own premises for industry events and training. Many professional associations will also allow reduced membership fees for students and there are even some associations that provide free memberships. You can often attend events as a visitor before deciding to join.

Professional associations generally offer Networking events, Job boards, Seminars, Conferences, Web resources,

Leadership opportunities, E-newsletters and Mentoring. By becoming an active member of a professional association, you have the opportunity of networking with enthusiastic professionals, including prospective future clients or employers. The benefits of professional networking groups include gaining more business and this can be worth the cost of membership alone. It is also an opportunity to hone ones people skills and learn more about people and their professionals and expand ones knowledge.

## Quality of Leads:

Leads obtained through networking, particularly through recommendations, will tend to be a higher quality lead producing higher quality business than general enquiries or solicited business. Such leads are usually:

Developed leads over time thorough the social networks,

Recommendations through network connections,

People who are interested in dealing with you or exchanging ideas and possibly business with you

Another advantage of such leads is the efficiency obtained thereby. Less advertising required means less cost required per lead so the ROI (return on investment) is greater. Less time is spent acquiring high quality leads and business and the risk management is improved with such savings as less risk of bad debt, time wasting on potential clients who turn out to be more time wasters than actual clients.

The reduction of time and money spent gaining new customers means more time can be spent on doing business and increasing profits.

It might be that you are in the fortunate position of having all the business you need right now, But in most cases business networking is not about the immediate increase of present day business but in setting up future business. Developing rapport and relationships with others takes time and is not a one-day activity with a 'buy now!' flavour attached to it. It is a relationship built on trust and mutual exchange of interests, ideas and referrals. It also tends to even out potential peaks and troughs in business. One might be at a peak now but very often a trough can appear and having some developed contacts that can provide you with a referral can help to fill that trough.

Being able to refer others to people you know they can trust is also a big feather in your cap. It improves their perception of you as a trustworthy individual and by reflection your company and increases your chances of being referred to others also. This is the peak of business networking and when one has reached this stage one will never be short of clients or customers.

## Establishing Networks:

Accessing quality services is made more possible through a portfolio of well-developed business network partners. If you are looking for a particular service, for example, which a current connection cannot provide, it is likely that one of your connection's can point you in the direction of someone that can provide that service. This can include potential discounts and savings thereby rather than having to seek out a company or professional you do not know and have received no recommendation for and would likely charge the top price for their service. By the same token there are advantages to offering discounts to referrals you have received as this is likely to increase the business you can obtain through business networking. Such mutual interchange can be a tremendous source of satisfaction, particularly if one is assisting new members to become more established, solve problems and start on the road to expansion. It makes one somewhat of a mentor in this regard.

Of course more knowledge and new skills can be acquired through networking associations including the opportunity to speak or make presentations at meetings. Such experiences help to develop more self-confidence with public speaking and increase the perception of you as a leader in your field. This leads into becoming an expert in your field. The more you meet on a regular basis with other professionals the greater awareness of business trends, developments and future directions you will have and this will enhance your reputation as being someone, 'in the know', or an expert in your chosen field.

Keeping up to date with trends will ensure that you are seen as being an expert fully up to date.

All these activities will go a long way to enhancing your reputation among professionals resulting in an increased confidence in you as a professional and expert and ultimately a person who whom referrals should be made. Your reputation for reliability and integrity would also be enhanced as the results of your recommendations reflect upon yourself.

## Maintaining Relationships:

Developing and building relationships is only the beginning. One cannot leave it there and say, "I have built a good relationship with Steve so need do nothing else." One needs to continuously maintain that relationship. This might mean contact on a regular basis, say once a week or month or every few months, depending on the relationship. Part of this is keeping you in the members mind, keeping you in the loop so to speak. Just developing a relationship and then not nurturing and not investing any quality time in the relationship means it will eventually deteriorate and, if you call say a year later and say, "Hi John, its Bill here."

The response might be, "Bill? Bill who?" Not a response you would be looking for.

Ways to maintain a relationship of this nature might include asking questions. Asking questions that call upon that individual's expertise. Of course if you ask someone who is very busy, you might get very short responses. But don't be discouraged! It is likely most of your business connections are busy. You are busy! So keep the questions short. Only ask question that you cannot answer or cannot find the answer on your own (asking questions, the answer to which can be found on Google, for example, is a prime example of a waste of time of yours and the person you are asking). Do not ask for the sake of asking. Questions very often end with a response that can open the door to further business opportunities.

Another way to keep in communication with your contacts is to send updates on matters you know or believe would interest them. People like to receive information that helps them keep up to date. Avoid the continual sending bad news however. Try to find constructive and positive information and news to send. Particularly as regards trends that concern them and their business. This can include industry updates for their industry. Apart from giving them information they may find valuable it also demonstrates an interest you have in their industry and business.

The key to networking is establishing contacts and developing a relationship before you need something from them. The last thing you want people to think is, *'He only contacts me when he wants something'*. Get what you want by helping others to get what they want first.

Building relationships takes time and effort. It is not a quick chat to someone you meet at a seminar and then get to do business with. By the same token a well-developed relationship can last years and have a mutual benefit to both parties in the years to come.

## Listening:

Listening is probably the highest respect one can pay to another. Hearing what they say and, vitally important, acknowledging them so they know that you have heard them is good communication.

Communication is not just what you talk about. It is also how you talk and listen to other people. Communication should be two way. Showing genuine interest in the other person and their business Finding out what services and benefits they offer can be just as important as telling them what you have to offer. After all, they just might have something that you want to need. It works both ways. You can spot opportunities this way. Find out what customers are they looking for, what contacts would be useful for them. Find out how you can help them and spot opportunities for them. Whether you are with friends and family or work colleagues, listen to what problems they have. Do you know someone who can solve that problem for them, providing them with a business opportunity?

Share your contacts with others. The names and details of contacts you trust and are reputable. Introduce people to each other. Build a reputation as someone with great contacts.

### Exceed Expectations:

Good service is giving what is expected. Great service is giving more than expected. Exceed expectations. The way to happiness for businesses is in keeping customers happy. The way to keep customers (emphasis on KEEP) is to exceed their expectations. Give more than they expect.

Look at customer service from the customer's point of view, what level of service does the customer expect or want?

THE CUSTOMER EXPECTS NOTHING LESS THAN PERFECT SERVICE OR THE BEST PRODUCT YOU CAN DELIVER

The customer always expects the best, regardless of the product or service offered. The customer does not expect to receive second best service. How many times have you jumped on a plane where it is announced the pilot was one of the second best pilots for the day? Or gone into a supermarket to buy your food and deliberately selected something that was half opened and shoddy looking and close to or past its use by date? Not very often I'm sure. This is what your customers do also. Many in fact make a point of looking for the use by date to ensure they pick the longest lasting product. This tells you the level of service and product quality and delivery you need to maintain in order to have satisfied customers and little or no complaints! It is not, how you talk to them or 'handle them'. That is not customer service.

Customer service is putting into place those steps and procedures required to ensure a quality product is delivered to your customer's door or an excellent service is fully delivered to your customer. That a follow up of some sort is made after the service or product is delivered to ensure your customer is satisfied and their expectations were met.

If the customer knows you deliver 'ujamaflips' on a 48-hour turn around and every time a coconut when he orders an 'ujamaflip' he gets it within 48 hours on his door step, he will be a happy customer. And if he gets a follow up call or email asking if everything is okay and did he get his 'ujamaflip' on time and in good condition? You will have an ecstatic customer who will stay with you forever. If your delivery is a hit or miss affair or the 'ujamaflip' turns out to be a 'duberedoo' instead, your customer will not be totally inspired by your ability to deliver what was promised. Then you will likely get a complaint, if you are lucky, or your competitor will get it if you are unlucky.

So customer service is not just listening or not arguing or being able to 'negotiate' with the customer. Although these are important, customer service includes those things you do before you have to listen or not argue or negotiate.

Ensure you have adequate stocks of your products. That they are up to scratch and work efficiently and are delivered on time and in the condition the customer expects them to be. Your service is exemplary and all-encompassing which is to say you leave nothing out. Ensure the customer is satisfied at every turn. Fully complete the service with no cut corners or skimping.

Going That Extra Mile

"A satisfied customer…we should have him stuffed."
– Basil Fawlty. ('Communications Problems.'
Fawlty Towers.)

For Basil Fawlty perhaps, a satisfied customer was a rarity hence the desire to have him stuffed for posterity. For you however it should be commonplace. Ideally all your customers should be satisfied. The success of a business most often depends on repeat business that is only obtainable from satisfied customers. So what is the best way to keep your customers forever? How can you generate fierce customer loyalty? How do you change a disgruntled customer who bitches and complains to all and sundry, to one that sings your praises to all who come within earshot?

You go that extra mile. That's how.

Well what does it mean going that extra mile? It means surprising the customer unexpectedly with a service that shows you care or are interested in them. Delivering in 24 hours what was expected within 48 is an example

Extending customer service beyond the customer's expectations.

Giving the irreducible service that one can 'get away with' is easily perceived by the customer. Customers can feel when they are being fobbed off or given the per functionary regulation service. Going that extra mile is doing more than that. When it is done well it is impressive and almost guaranteed to capture a customer forever. If you can extend your customer service beyond the customer's expectations, you will have a customer for life. But what can you do to give your customers an extended customer service that goes beyond your customer's expectations? Being the Rolls Royce of customer service and making the customer feel important is a good start. Guess how Rolls Royce customers are treated? Roll out the metaphorical red carpet for all customers. How would you feel if you were treated this way? You would be a customer for life!

The New York Times best-selling author Steven Levitt wrote an article about how United Airlines turned him into a customer for life in a couple ways. Steven was running late and unlike other airlines, they actually saved his seat until the last second. On another occasion, United Airlines called him and informed him that his flight was delayed by a few hours and they saw that he was in the airport. The call went like this:

"I see that you're at the airport and your flight is delayed a few hours. A seat opened up on an earlier flight, so I grabbed it for you in case you wanted it. It leaves in 40 minutes, so you'll have to hurry." These two events, Levitt explains, turned him into a life-long customer of United Airlines.

And another customer, "I had a fault on my phone line so I reported it to my service supplier, who got onto BT Open reach to get the fault fixed. I reported the fault on the Friday morning, my service supplier's customer service called me back five times on the Friday to let me know how they were proceeding with my fault, the fault was fixed on the Saturday and I got three calls the next week from my company just checking that everything was working properly again. I considered that brilliant service."

It can be a profound change of attitude for some companies to move from giving the 'irreducible minimal' needed to finding ways of giving more than expected in order to retain customers. Guess which produces the most loyal customers and best results?

This applies in no small measure to your contacts and developing relationships. Treat them as customers, even if they are not. In reality they are customers who have not yet bought your product or service.

## Gaining Trust and Confidence

If a potential contact does not trust you or have any confidence in you, then they will never be a contact and a relationship will never develop so how do you gain trust and confidence? Trust is a firm belief in someone or something. What can you do that would foster trust in you by another? The first and foremost way to gain trust is to demonstrate honesty and openness. Being you and not putting up a false image of yourself. People do not buy from the first person they contact. They buy from people they can trust. Building rapport and demonstrating credibility as the relationship develops. Three areas can help with building trust.

Knowing about the person you are developing a relationship with and having them know you very well also.

Communication with good quality listening and developing a rapport with someone genuinely liking them and appreciating them as an individual

These three factors built up together will encourage a greater understanding in the relationship and bring you closer together where trust and credibility will develop. Building trust does not stop at mere introductions or getting acquainted with someone. It extends further. It develops more over time and is, to be honest, directly proportional to the amount of effort one puts into the relationship. One might gain a small sale out of a relationship after a period of time. This is not the time to relax. This is the time to continue developing the relationship and the trust factor by providing excellent customer service and committee demonstrations of honestly and reliability.

## Building Rapport:

Having a genuine and not false interest in someone is the first step to building rapport. When a person has more rapport with you, they will want to know more about you and the level of communication increases, they find you more interesting and a relationship is built.

Here are some useful hints on building rapport with another.

Make eye contact and smile.

Introduce yourself using your first name only and politely ask theirs.

Repeat their name. Apart from fixing it in your memory, it always makes people feel good hearing their name. One can start by asking natural questions, such as, 'have you been to these events before?' 'who do you know here?' And of course, 'what do you do?' Look for 'ideas or interests in common' to talk about. Perhaps there are people you know in common, or who work in the same industry or your businesses are related Ask further questions related to what the other person has said which demonstrates you are listening and that you are interested in what they are saying

Listen and show that you are listening.

Build on what they have said e.g. "Yes, I can see how that would be challenging. I've had a similar situation myself. If it helps at all, I would be happy to share how I handled it…"

Ask for their business card and make related comments "Ah yes, I have heard of your company before. How long have you been established?"

Always keep your comments positive. 'Mirror' their body language. This is one of the most interesting business networking skills. Research has shown that people form closer bonds to those that mirror their body language. However, do not try to copy everything. If the person has a 'tic', for example, I strongly suggest NOT mirroring that tic. If the person is aware they have a tic, they may consider you are poking fun at them. If they are not, they may think there is something wrong with you. Practice on friends and relations if this aspect is unfamiliar with you and see what results you get.

Some final tips

Here are some final tips on Business Networking:

Tuning in to your clients or prospects is important and to recap here are some final points worth noting,

Listening (again),

Listening is so important it is iterated here once again. Listening with understanding and empathy, also called active listening, is also important to find out who your prospect is and what motivates them. What are they seeking? Do they have an issue you can help them with? In order to know this one needs the information so asking open-ended questions and listening carefully to the answers or responses is most important.

One point here that is sometimes overlooked. Separate the process of taking information in from any judgement. Focus on understanding them and their business. One can sometimes be surprised by what one finds out this way. Things are not always as they first seem.

Let your contact tell their story first. This might be difficult if your contact has the same idea and is trying to get your story first. The simple way to handle this is to answer any question completely and honestly asked of you and then immediately ask a question in return. Practice controlling the conversation. Use head nodding and acknowledgements and open-ended questions.

The use of acknowledgement to let the other person know that you heard and understood them is important. Even to the point of paraphrasing back to them your understanding of what they are talking about and confirming that is correct if required.

An important point that, if a client is telling you about a problem they are having and no immediate solution comes to mind then it is quite possible you do not have all the information. Continue to ask questions and dig further. Sometimes, what you are being told will change with each question or query and then the solution may come to light. When this happens, your altitude will soar in the mind of your client and you will become an authority figure.

## Committing:

If you state you will do something, offer some help or advice or some form of support, DO IT. Action does not speak louder than words. It screams. Always follow through on any commitment made, no matter how inconvenient it turns out to be. Always keep any promise made. Demonstrate being a 'man of your word'. This builds trust and respect and offers a level of professionalism that will stand you in good stead in the years to come.

## Negotiating:

A time will come when you have the opportunity to negotiate with your contacts and business relationships. Sometimes not just with regards to sales and services but to the business relationship itself. This can extend to such mundane things as 'finders fees' for referrals and the like. If this type of activity is potentially on the table, it is important to get the agreements all squared away as soon as a business relationship has been developed.

Negotiation is the activity of two or more parties determining the value and agreement of exchange between the parties concerned. Such arrangements, which it must be said should always be within the law, can be an exchange of services or products that equate to a 'quid pro quo' basis.

The important factors in negotiations are:

Communication
Understanding
Agreement

Out of the three, communication is the most senior and the most important since it is the one that controls the other two. Having specific, open and informed communication leads to understanding and agreement.

One cannot have understanding and agreement between parties without the communication factor. Therefore one's communication must be of the highest quality, clear and concise and relevant to the subject at hand. It should contain no unrelated emotion and definitely no criticism or an unprofessional quality regarding other or another.

Each negotiation is a separate activity to any other negotiation. The circumstances, people and subject are going to be unique to that particular negotiation and, although the basics of negotiation remain the same, the subject matter, intentions and desires will be different with each negotiation. One is dealing with people each of whom has come to the negotiating table with their own radio station, WII FM (What's in it for me).

So it is entirely possible that negotiations may take more than one round to reach a satisfactory level or stage for all concerned. Because no satisfactory result was obtained in the first round does not mean that one throws ones hands in the air and forgets all about it. One can look for ways to continue the negotiations such as, what else can I bring to the table the other party or parties want?

Here are some points that can help towards a successful negotiation in the business network situation:

- Importantly, a basis for communication among the parties, including the ability to understand the importance's of culture, language and the resources available to meet together,
- The ability to 'read' the other party's speech and body-signals in meetings and the ability to cope with conflict and emotion,
- The authority and power of all parties to commit to and deliver or the agreed arrangements,
- Parties who are, or at least may be, capable of agreeing on a negotiation,
- Mutual recognition and respect among the parties,
- Interest by the parties in achieving an outcome.

A successful negotiator needs to develop knowledge, skills and strategies that will enhance the process to deliver positive outcomes. This includes an understanding and acceptance of the various cultures and mindsets one might meet in business today as well as the ability to apply superior communication skills such as active listening and verbal skills.

A negotiator should have self-confidence and be able to apply assertive behaviours, without becoming aggressive yet remain cool, robust and resilient under pressure. He should also apply patience and flexibility.

He should have the ability to understand proposals and their implications and be able to offer effective counter proposals.

A successful negotiator always starts a negotiation with collaboration in mind. This helps to avoid missing a potential immediate and advantageous solution, a win-win solution for all parties. Using consensus and collaboration with the intention in mind of creating a mutually rewarding agreement and result will also create a long-term relationship.

## Finally:

The solution to potential problems and difficult situations and conflicts in negotiation or, indeed, in any developing business networking relationship is more communication not less. Communication is a universal solvent and continuing to communicate, with oneself initiating or getting another party to talk about their issues can, more often than not, lead to a solution to the issue at hand. One can then work through any problems systematically to a solution that satisfies all parties.

Applying the previously mentioned skills and workthrough brings more clarity and understanding. If you do not understand or see the problem they are having, get them to explain it more fully. Find out what they truly want. Even questions such as, "What goals did you have in mind when we started?" or "Where do you want to go from here?" "What will success look like to you?" or "What do you feel your options are for the future?" can also often help to gain some clarity not just for oneself but sometimes for the other party.

Sometimes, when we are working with potential clients, there can be too many problem-solving conversations with the focus on the past or on what was done.

Each party having a goal or purpose in mind and focusing on that can make a big difference in how the negotiation is broached and the result. A good question both parties can ask themselves is: "What can I bring to the negotiating table that will enhance the future prosperity of both parties?" Focusing on solutions, ideal scenarios, what will help the negotiating be a rewarding experience for all parties and will lead to success in negotiation resulting in the future prosperity of all parties.

And remember, if the negotiation becomes tough, more communication, not less, is the answer every time.

# Customer Service

A company's customers are its lifeblood. And the contact point between a company and its customers is customer service. Much has been written about customer service but to gain an increased understanding of customer service let's put it the other way around. Instead of saying customer service, let's say servicing the customer. The importance of servicing the customer becomes then, the quality of service given to the customer. Service is defined as 'the action of helping, assisting or doing something for someone'. In this case a customer.

A customer is one who buys or exchanges goods or may potentially buy or exchange services from you. The question then becomes, what quality of customer service is appropriate to give?

Should it be the economically irreducible minimal the company can afford? Or should it be giving service to the point where the customer's expectations are exceeded in their own estimation? Or is it somewhere in between?

As a guide to servicing the customer, there are three principles that can help here.

### Principle 1:

The customer always considers they are right.

No customer has ever considered they are wrong. Even if they say they are, deep down they still consider they are right. In Asia a guiding principle is that the customer is King.

## Principle 2:

The customer always considers they are top or first priority.

No customer ever said, "I am second priority." No customer ever jumped on a plane where it was announced "the pilot for this flight is our second (third, fourth) best pilot, but he is very good considering."

And any passengers on such a plane, on hearing that announcement prior to take off, would be fighting to get off the moment that announcement was heard.

## Principle 3:

The customer holds the whip hand.

The customer has the final 'weapon of mass destruction'. He or she can always, at any time during the sale or negotiation, say that dreaded word. NO.

The only criteria that can satisfy all three principles are the qualities of service given to a customer or client that treats the customer as if he were right.

Makes it plain, that he or she is your top or first priority and makes it hard if not impossible to say no.

Wikipedia explains Customer service as being the provision of service to customers before, during and after a purchase. According to Turban et al. "Customer service is a series of activities designed to enhance the level of customer satisfaction – that is, the feeling that a product or service has met the customer expectation." According to some people, the importance of customer service may vary by product or service, industry and customer. However I beg to differ as this, to me, implies that a situation where less than the very best customer service may be justified. It also would violate the three principles above.

Customer service or servicing the customer can be broken down into five steps or actions.

Getting in communication with a customer or client

Finding out what the customer wants and/or needs by listening to the customer and asking questions.

Finding a way in which that want or need can be serviced or filled.

Getting the customer to see that this is the solution to his or her want or need. Presenting this solution to the customer in such a way that they see this is the best solution that benefits them and they want it.

Investopedia explains 'Customer Service' as "an extremely important part of maintaining on-going client relationships that are the key to continuing revenue." This means that servicing the customer does not stop with the first sale or solution offered to the customer. Servicing is an on-going activity. It does not mean also demanding the customer filled out a feedback form. It is nice if a customer does fill out such a form. It can help the company or business gauge the quality of service being offered and point the company in the direction of improving their service level. But a feedback form is for the benefit of the company, not for the customer and is NOT part of servicing the customer. Likewise, testimonials. Success stories etc.

Follow up calls come under the category of continuing customer service. Asking the customer if they were satisfied and if there is any further service or product that can be offered comes under the banner of servicing the customer.

Speed of service also comes under the banner of customer service. How fast can one provide the service or product? How quick is the company's response to queries, questions and complaints?

How easy is it to communicate with the company without spending hours waiting on the phone or seeking a contact web page?

And when a customer finally contacts a person in the company, how helpful are they? Do they not just listen but also hear what the customer is saying? And does their response reflect that to the customer's satisfaction.

Many companies treat after sales service as a necessary pain. This is reflected in some call centres who have performance indicators that do not reflecting how satisfied the customer is but rather how short the call can be made so more calls can be taken by each phone operator resulting in less staff needed. Customers can be discouraged by long waits and big queues. In one call centre, for example, calls of five minutes or over are discouraged and operators can be severely upbraided if their calls take longer as a rule. The result being that the operator is more interested in meeting his performance targets than in giving quality service to the customer. And make no mistake, no matter how polite an operator can be, a customer can tell when they are being rushed or when the operator wants to 'wind up the call' even slightly.

These reflect a lesser quality of servicing the customer. This comes under the irreducible minimum service offered in that will retain the customer at an effective economical cost to the company. It also violates principle two above.

A company striving to exceed the customer expectations with service will achieve far more and be much more successful than one focused on reducing costs and treating service as a necessary evil. Remembering and using the three principles above will go a long way to increasing the customer base and the success of the company or business.

Another way of increasing brand loyalty to the point of a customer never leaving or churning from their current to another brand is by introducing a policy of going that extra mile.

Well what does it mean, going that extra mile? It means surprising the customer unexpectedly with a service that shows you care or are interested in them. It means extending customer service beyond the customer's expectations.

Giving the irreducible minimum service that one can 'get away with' is easily perceived by the customer. Customers can feel when they are being fobbed off or given the per functionary regulation service.

Going that extra mile is doing more than that. When it is done well, it is impressive and almost guaranteed to ensure brand loyalty and capture a customer forever.

This applies to complaints as well. Instead of viewing complaints as a necessary evil, how about as a stepping-stone to increasing customer loyalty and retention?

In short, if you can extend your customer service beyond the customer's expectations you will have a customer for life.

And that is something any organisation these days would be keenly interested in I'm sure.

# Reading Financial Statements for Directors

A vital and important part of a director's duty is to guide, monitor and understand the financials of an organisation. A director is considered responsible, even liable, for the viability and financial well-being of the company on each board he or she sits. This means they are legally accountable and there can be serious consequences for a board of directors who do not take such responsibility seriously.

This being said, it must be that the financial reports and records presented to the board should be understood well by the board and the board able to use the reports as part of their governance in running the organisation and ensuring that management is managing the company effectively. The three principle financial records or statements the board need to consider are:

Income Statement
Balance Sheet and
Cash Flow Statement

### Income Statement:

This is a summary of the income and expenses from the first day to the last day of the reporting period. It shows in list form, the gross income less the expenses to arrive at the profit (or loss) before tax. It also shows this figure less tax to leave a balance of Net profit (profit after expenses and tax).

The simple formula for the Income Statement is:
I - E = P
I = income and sometimes called revenue and even earnings for an individual.
E = Expenses and
P = Profit.

So, it is simply income less expenses resulting in profit.

For most organisations, sales of products and or services are the most common source of income or revenue. This is usually when the goods are shipped or the service delivered. Other income can include royalties, commissions etc. Expenses are those items incurred as part of the activity to generate income. This can include salaries, annual leave, rent, utilities etc.

These expenses may not bare any immediate relationship to the income earned but are nevertheless valid expenses required in order to participate in the activities needed to earn the income. For example, rent. One requires a location from which to operate, a shop, factory place of business from which products and or services are sold and income is earned.

A proper breakdown of income and expenses is necessary for management and directors to understand and monitor the performance of the organisation.

Commonly a typical format for this would be:

Sales
Less: cost of goods sold
Gives: gross profit
Less: selling expenses
Less: administrative expenses
Add: other revenue
Gives: profit before tax.

The complexity of this will increase in relation to the size of the organisation. Where an organisation is a large retail chain it will then, have two major functions, warehousing and distribution and these would need to be included either before or after gross profit. Each outlet would have their own profit and loss and the total would result in the overall gross profit for the organisation. The larger the organisation the more reporting and breakdown of income and expenses would need to be included to show the profit and loss of each area.

Service organisations are a little different in that they do not usually have inventory but in those exceptions where you do, there would again be a cost of goods sold and a gross profit.

This then would be:

Sales
Less: cost of goods sold consisting of:
Opening inventory.
Add: purchases, direct labour, manufacturing overheads for a manufacturer.
Less: closing inventory.
Gives: cost of goods sold.
Gives: gross profit.

So there is a link between the income statement and the balance sheet. The closing inventory is taken from the goods sold as it is still there at the end of the financial year and so is an asset. This can affect the year's profit.

The more the closing inventory is considered to be worth, the lower the cost of goods sold and the higher the gross profit and profit before tax. So it is important to get the value of the inventory at years end accurate.

The Australian Accounting Standards Board (AASB) defines income and expenses as:

Income is increases in economic benefits during the accounting period in the form of inflows or enhancements of assets or decreases of liabilities that result in increases in equity, other than those relating to contributions from equity participants. [Paragraph 70(a)]

Expenses are decreases in economic benefits during the accounting period in the form of outflows or depletions of assets or incurrences of liabilities that result in decreases in equity, other than those relating to distribution to equity participants. [Paragraph 70(b)]

Sometimes there are unusual or one-off types of items that can distort the final figures and which, without being recorded, would not allow a proper prospective to apply to the figures for management purposes. However, all items, unusual or not, must be included in any reports.

AASB, 101, paragraph 86 advises that "when items of income and expenses are material, their nature and amount shall be disclosed separately." The term 'material' is defined in paragraph 11 as:

Omissions or miss-statements of items are material if they could individually or collectively, influence the economic decisions of users taken on the basis of the financial report. Materiality depends on the size and nature of the omission or miss-statement judged in the surrounding circumstances. The size or nature of the item, or a combination of both could be a determining factor.

Note also, that what were once called 'extraordinary items' are now called material items.

Taxable income is different from profit. Taxable income is defined in section 4-15 of the Australian Income Tax Assessment Act 1997 as:

Assessable income less allowable deductions

The profit before income tax is different to the taxable income in that there are disparities between the two.

Such differences can be the result of:

Depreciation
Capital expenditures
Provisions for long service and annual leave.
Qualifying expenditure

Depreciation rates can vary between companies. Whereas a small company may use the standard tax schedule rates a larger company may have different rates.

Capital expenditures may or may not be allowed as a deduction depending upon what it is and the circumstances.

Provisions for annual leave and long service leave are expenses occurred but would, not be tax deductible until the leave is taken or paid out.

Qualifying expenditure can change the tax rates and what is paid also. Expenditure on research and development can attract a larger deduction than the cost of the expenditure itself.

The other factor that can influence the tax paid is deferred taxes. Deferred taxes are those taxes one expects to pay when a profit is realised from say, the sale of an asset. Deferred tax assets (DTA) are the amounts of income taxes which are recoverable in future periods of deductible temporary differences, such as carrying forward unused tax loses and carrying forward unused tax credits.

But a deferred tax asset is only recognised if it is considered probable that tax benefit will be realise in the future.

A director needs to make himself familiar with the basic tax principles and rules when reading any income statement and balance sheet. Particularly when it comes to assets and the tax considerations, thereof.

Levels of profit are usually expressed as:

EBITDA = earnings before interest, tax, depreciation and amortisation
Less: Depreciation and amortisation
Gives: EBIT = earnings before interest and tax
Less: Interest
Gives: EBT = earnings before tax (called 'profit before tax' in some accounting systems)
Less: Tax

Gives: E = earnings (called 'net profit' and often referred to a NPAT, 'net profit after tax' – a term not generally used these days in accounting)

### Balance Sheet:

This shows also in list form, what the organisation owns less what it owes. The balance is the equity of the organisation at the last date of the reporting period. This would be total assets, both current and non-current, less any liabilities both current and non-current. The balance is the net assets or equity of the organisation.

The balance sheet, or statement of financial position as it is called now, shows the assets, liabilities and equity at a particular time. Usually, the $30^{th}$ of June in Australia being the end of the fiscal year.

The Balance sheet can be expressed in a formula where A = assets, L = liabilities and E = Equity.

The formula, then, used is L + E = A

The owner's interest in the organisation can also be expressed as:

E = A - L

A good example is where one purchases a property. Let's say the property was purchased for one million dollars.

The deposit was 250,000 and the borrowing was 750,000. At the start of the term the asset is worth one million dollars and the liability 750,000 leaving equity of 250,000. A year later, as payments are made, the situation changes. Let's say an addition 200,000 was paid. Also, the value of the property increased by 10%.

One would have a liability of 550,000, an asset of 1,100,000 and an equity now of 550,000.

You have increase equity in the property of 100,000 as well as the contribution you made. This is called a revaluation gain. The equity therefore consists, in this simple example, of contributions made over the time period and any change in the value of the asset.

Equity does not include cash. Cash is only realised if an asset is sold, whereas then it would come of the balance sheet as equity and be considered as cash at bank, or cash holdings for example.

Equity is simply the assets held less any liabilities or in other words what is left when you deduct the liabilities from the assets. A good definition of an asset is, "Something owned" either by an individual or a company or an entity. One purchases or buys assets and one can sell assets. Another definition for asset is, "something owned which can produce a value in the future."

Liabilities are the other side of the coin however. A definition of a liability is, "Something owed as a result of something that has occurred." A mortgage is a liability. It is something owed as a result of a purchase of property.

Liability is defined by the AASB as:

A liability is a present obligation of the entity arising from past events, the settlement of which is expected to result in an outflow from the entity of resources embodying economic benefits. (Paragraph 49[b]).

Liabilities can be divided in current and non-current.

Current liabilities include:

Accounts payable: These are also called creditors. These are those entities that the company owes money to for value received. This can be suppliers as well as accruals. An accrual is something accrued. I.e. a benefit is expected to be received, either goods or services which have not yet been paid for and so the debt is accrued. E.g. Electricity or gas. The benefit is expected and the cost is accrued but not paid for.

Borrowings: Using other funds or money than owned by the entity and for which payments, in the form of interest and loan fees are due. Loans, overdrafts, commercial bills are examples. Provisions are similar to accruals.

The AASB has defined an asset as follows:

An asset is a resource controlled by the entity as a result of past events and from which future economic benefits are expected to flow to the entity. (paragraph 49(a)).

Directors are the stewards of the organisations assets and have a duty to ensure they are treated in such a way that asset value is added to and maintained by the organisation. A director, therefore, needs to be satisfied that an asset actually exists and is valued appropriately and not over or under valued. It should be born in mind that while some assets may increase in value over a period others may decrease or be amortised. Some assets, such as intangibles like good will etc., can only be reported at cost. Assets are show on the balance sheet as either current or non-current assets. Current means that that asset will be converted into cash or another asset or will be used up within the 12 months from the balance sheet date. Any other assets are classified as non-current.

The most common current assets you might find on a balance sheet are:

Cash: Cash holdings such as you might find in a bank and cash on hand such as petty cash for example.

Receivables: Funds owed by debtors to the organisation from other parties. Trade debtors are the most common.

These are funds owned by customers who have been sold a product or service on credit.

Inventories: This is the stock of products purchased for resale but not yet sold.

Prepayments: This is where a client or customer pays in advance for a product or service to be received. Insurance is a good example.

Non-current assets found on a balance sheet are:

Investments: These are sometimes also labelled as 'other financial assets' and could be called savings for a rainy day. These include investments in shares, interest bearing securities, or investment properties for example:

Property, plant and equipment. These are also called fixed assets. They can include, land, buildings, plant, equipment, cars computers, furniture etc. Materials required for the organisation to produce its services or goods for resale.

Intangibles. Good will, trade or brand names, trademarks, patents and the like.

Deferred tax assessment, which arises from the way income tax is accounted for as compared to how it is assessed under the tax laws.

Some non-current assets would be depreciated or amortised. Cars, computers and furniture, for example. Others may increase in value, such as goodwill.

Assets need to be valued on a regular basis to ensure fair value. It is easy to over value assets just as it is easy to under value them. The fair value should be assessed annually.

## Cash Flow Statement:

This shows the flow of cash or money through the organisations from the first to the last day of the period being counted or reported on. Again in list form this would be the total receipts less any payments to equal the net operating activities. Also receipts less any payments to show a balance of net investing activities. And receipts less any net financing activities to equal a net cash increase (or decrease). Then add cash at the beginning to give a total of the cash at the end of the reporting period.

The simple formula for the Cash Flow Statement is:

Cash at the beginning of the period
Add: cash receipts
Less: cash payments
Gives: cash at the end of the period
Of course, it invariably ends up more complex than this as other factors enter into it. For example:
Net cash from operating activities
Add: net cash from investing activities
Add: net cash from financing activities
Gives: net change in cash for the period
Add: cash at the beginning of the period
Gives: cash at the end of the period

Some other examples of cash flows from operating activities:

Cash receipts/ inflows Cash payments/ outflows receipts from customers payments to suppliers and employees' dividends received interest paid interest received Income tax paid of course the cash received from customers should be larger than the payments to suppliers and employees otherwise the company is heading for trouble,

Cash Flows from investing activities,

Cash receipts / inflows Cash payments / outflows,

Proceeds from disposal of property, Payments for purchase of property,

Plant and equipment plant and equipment,

Proceeds from sale of investments payment for investments,

Proceeds from sale of companies payments for purchases of companies and businesses.

Sometimes, these days, a company will find it more economical and tax advantageous to lease rather than buy and tie up funds in capital

Cash Flows from financing activities,

Cash receipts / inflows Cash payments / outflows,

Proceeds from issue of shares Return of capital/share buyback,

Dividends received Dividends paid,

Proceeds from new borrowings repayment of principal on borrowings,

Note: there are some cash flow warning signals to look for. Three of them are:
Net profit cash outflows (negative operating cash flows), Payments to suppliers and employees are higher than receipts from customers and
Net operating cash flows are lower than profit after tax.

If any two are found to be present, then directors should be alerted as this can be a warning that insolvency is potentially looming.

A difference between the income Statement and cash Flow statement is that income and expenses are recognised when they incurred while cash and payments are recognised when they are received and paid.

Cash can be received for a sale either before, during or after the sale is made. In a supermarket, the cash is paid at the same time the goods are delivered to the customer. In a credit situation the cash is paid after the goods are delivered and in some situations (mail order or insurance for example) the cash is paid before the goods are delivered.

A separate report these days is required for a change in equity and comprehensive income.

The statement should include:

The total comprehensive income

All transactions between the entity and its owners, typically being such things as dividends, share issues, buy backs and returns of capital.

The statement should show the opening balance of each, any transactions, such as gains, losses, transfers etc. and then the closing balance for each.

Notes to the Accounts:

These go further in providing additional detailed information to the data presented in a report and should be read, not skipped over, by the directors. These are usually numbered one (1) through to the total number of notes presented and each will often give extensive information, regarding that element or figure in the accounts. They can show a very enlightened view not immediately apparent in the three basic reports.

The first note is usually a statement of the financial or accounting policies used by the company. Subsequent notes might cover such matters as:

Significant other party transactions
Market value of assets and liabilities
Interest rates
Currency rates and significant changes
One off extraordinary items

Reporting of various areas, such as geographical or business segments, subsidiaries and associated companies.

## Analysing Financial Reports:

Each report shows a difference aspect of the company's financial activities. The income statement shows how much income is being made less the expenses incurred in making that income, the balance sheet shows how much equity the company owns and the cash flow statement shows the flow of money through the organisation.

Most important for a director is to ensure that compliance with the various regulatory accounting standards are being in effect. This is where committees for larger companies assist. Committees to monitor and ensure compliance with the various laws and guidelines imposed on companies and on board members. The board has a duty to ensure the company is complying with the various regulations and there can be stiff penalties where a board has been remiss in this. If a director cannot show they have done all they can to ensure legal compliance, then they can face fines and even imprisonment.

Setting the financial risk for the company is an important factor also for the board to consider. The director should want to be able to monitor risk as it applies to the purposes and objectives of the company.

Lastly, the board is accountable to the shareholders and should be reporting progress and matters of interest to the shareholders. This might include the direction the board is taking with regard to the company, any change of direction, any acquisition or divestment of a significant asset and full disclosure of matters which the board consider are significant to report to the shareholders.

I hope this little booklet has been of assistance in navigating the world of company directorship and you have a wonderful productive tenure as a corporate company director.

# References

INCORP SERVICES, INC. *Glossary of Corporate Terms* [Online] Las Vegas, NV, USA, 04 FEB 2020
https://www.incorp.com/help-center/glossary

THE FREE DICTIONARY, *Punc-til-i-ous* [Online] Farlex, Inc. Huntington Valley, Pennsylvania, USA, 04 FEB 2020
https://www.thefreedictionary.com/punctilious

DEPARTMENT OF LOCAL GOVERNMENT, SPORT AND CULTURAL INDUSTRIES, GOVERNMENT OF WESTERN AUSTRALIA, *Sports and Recreation* [Online] Perth, WA, 04 FEB 2020
https://www.dlgsc.wa.gov.au/sport-and-recreation

JACOBS. S, THOMSEN. S, BUSINESS INSIDER AUSTRALIA, *FIRST STRIKE! AMP shareholders revolt in the biggest corporate rebuke in Australian history* [Online] May 10, 2018, 04 FEB 2020
https://www.businessinsider.com.au/amp-annual-general-meeting-first-strike-2018-5

AMP, Share price graph [Online] Melbourne, 04 FEB 2020, 04 FEB 2020, https://corporate.amp.com.au/shareholder-centre/shareholder-info/share-price-graph

DANCKERT. S, THE SUNDAY MORNING HERALD Three AMP directors step down amid investor outcry [Online] Sydney, Australia, May 8, 2018, 04 FEB 2020
https://www.smh.com.au/business/banking-and-

finance/amp-directors-step-down-ahead-of-meeting-20180508-p4zdyv.html

https://www.aasb.gov.au/

https://www.companydirectors.com.au/
eprints.usq.edu.au/1401/1/Eddington_Searle_Temple-Smith_AWBMMD.pdf

luc.edu/law/faculty/ramirez/pdfs/flaw_sarbanes.pdf

wikipedia.org/wiki/Cultural_lag

http://www.companydirectors.com.au/

Duties and Responsibilities of Directors and Officers Professor Bob Baxt AO 19th Edition

https://www.companydirectors.com.au/

https://www.asic.gov.au/asic/ASIC.NSF/byHeadline/Company%20_compliance

https://www.accc.gov.au/content/index.phtml/itemId/365

https://www.behanlegal.com/KnowledgeCentre/CompaniesCorporationsLaw/DirectorsDutiesResponsibilities/tabid/149/Default.aspx

en.wikipedia.org/wiki/Six_degrees_of_separation

A Glossary of terms for directors can be found at:

https://www.companydirectors.com.au/~/media/resources/director-resource-centre/publications/books/pdfsvarious/Glossary-Language-of-Directorship-Feb-2013.ashx